SOUL MATES *by* GOD

A 31-DAY JOURNEY
WITH
THE MATCHMAKER

Brad and Nicole Tabian

myPraize, Inc.

A 31-Day Journey with the Matchmaker
Soul Mates *by* God

Published by myPraize, Inc.
1900 32nd Ave. NE
Black Eagle, MT 59414

Details in some anecdotes and stories have been changed or combined for ease of reading and/or to protect the identities of the persons involved.

The names Brad and Nicole Tabian are pseudonyms.

ISBN: 9781688776364

SoulMatesByGod.com
SoulMates@myPraize.com

CONTENTS

APPENDIX

PREFACE
A NEW PERSPECTIVE

Does God really have a custom-designed mate for you? We all have situations in life where we find ourselves coming up to a wall. We can't figure out how to get around it nor can we see any potential for good in the situation. And yet, if we step to the side where there is no wall blocking our view, we can see possibilities.

Soul Mates by God is designed as a tool with which you learn to see and then experience life from this different angle. Not one of frustration or worry or fear or loneliness. Our goal is that you learn to look at your life from God's perspective. He sees you as his wonderful creation and is enjoying your journey as you trek through life and through the transformation process with him. Your journey to a soul mate is one strewn with treasure along the way, gifts to spiritually adorn yourself with before you meet your partner. We can choose to be fearful or anxious, or we can learn to enjoy the process with him.

For me (Nicole), dating was always a roller coaster experience. There was the thrill of being on the "ride," but was there love around the corner? Was the initial compatibility I felt on those first dates going to continue or was I once again going to have to face disappointment?

It wasn't until I had started seeing my life as a journey with God that the pressure of performance in my dating life changed. I began to realize that each person I dated was a gift to me. I was learning facts about myself, that didn't always make me look good. As a result, I was having to face and deal with them. I didn't know how many of these experiences God was going to take me through to prepare me for my soul mate.

I learned to trust God and to enjoy the relationships I was experiencing. Even if the relationship didn't go the distance, it wasn't because I was "broken" or that the one I was dating was "bad." It just wasn't a match for me or them. And thank God he ended each one of those relationships. Because the best was yet to come—Brad.

Nicole

INTRODUCTION
THE JOURNEY BEGINS

"Matchmaker, matchmaker, make me a match, find me a find, catch me a catch." You may remember the words to this well-known song from the 1970's classic musical, *Fiddler on the Roof*. The story follows three daughters of a Jewish family whose parents desire to match them up with a "perfect" match. Various predicaments are encountered by everyone involved, and since this isn't your life, you can laugh (and cry) about the various difficulties and dilemmas.

But seriously, are those lyrics your heart's desire? Do you want someone to help you identify the right person that you can share the rest of your life with?

You want to be married, but how is that going to happen? Will your family or friends help you find your ideal soul mate? Perhaps you intend to make your own match? Where does God fit in? Does he?

Matchmaking has been going on since the beginning of human-kind. But how it is done varies from culture to culture and age to age. Most commonly, marriages have been arranged by parents. More recently it is through online dating websites. But no matter where or when, there have always been professional matchmakers who can be employed by the affluent to arrange the perfect marriage for their offspring.

Historically, a good matchmaker had several responsibilities:

1. The matchmaker needed to be motivated enough to get involved in creating a match.

2. The matchmaker needed to understand the desires, characteristics, and circumstances of the person needing a match.

3. The matchmaker needed to have the ability to go wherever necessary in order to search for an appropriate person to fit the situation.

4. Once the matchmaker found a good match, the two people had to be brought together so they could meet each other.

5. And once they met, the matchmaker helped guide the relational discovery process that would ultimately lead to marriage.

Do you realize God is the ultimate Matchmaker? Unlike the matchmakers from the past, whose goal was to match people for the sake of preserving society and promoting a lasting heritage, the ultimate Matchmaker is about pairing up couples to fulfill the purpose for which they were created. His pairing is not only based on who you are, but also on who he wants you to become. He has promised, that as a believer, he will provide everything you need to live the life he desires for you here on earth while participating in the building of his eternal kingdom.

God has been matchmaking since the beginning of creation.

- He custom-designed Eve to be a perfect fit for Adam (Genesis 2:21–22).
- He used Abraham's servant to find a wife for Isaac. She then became the love of Isaac's life (Genesis 24).
- He opened Boaz's eyes to see Ruth's wonderful qualities before Boaz chose to make her his wife (Ruth 2–3).

God can do the same for you.

Do you want to enlist the services from the ultimate Matchmaker and discover his best for you?

Every devotional in this book reveals an important truth that you need for this journey—31 keys to help you become your best so you are ready to meet God's best for you. Make it a priority to prayerfully reflect on each unit and then truthfully answer the questions from the Matchmaker. Once you have completed this 31-day journey, go through the devotions a second time. During this second month of review, focus on what has changed? Would you answer any of the Matchmaker's questions differently after the first month of having your thoughts transformed?

This is the journey only you can take with the Matchmaker. He is waiting to be your guide. Let God be your Matchmaker.

The journey begins ...

PART 1

Your Relationship

with

the Matchmaker

Day 1
Partnering with the Matchmaker

Ah, Sovereign LORD, you have made the heavens and the earth
by your great power and outstretched arm. Nothing is too hard for you.
Jeremiah 32:17, NIV

Congratulations as you begin your journey with God to find a soul mate! Your most important step in seeking the right marriage partner is choosing God to be your Matchmaker.

Most people, if they are honest, believe that they know what is best for themselves. And so, they search for a soul mate without seeing the need to involve anyone else in the process. They don't realize that left to their own devices, the likelihood of making an excellent choice is not very probable.

Why? Because of their personal limitations. Among other things, their knowledge, foresight, and objectivity are usually short-sighted as well as compromised because of their emotions. I've also found that many people tend to make short lists so that their current date has a better chance of making the grade.

Then there are those individuals who do seek help from family and friends or a googled resource on the Internet. While they have broadened the scope of their search, all of these additional resources also have limitations.

By trusting God to be your Matchmaker, you have connected with the ultimate best source for finding a soul mate. God has NO limitations.

Consider God's infinite abilities. He is all-powerful, sees everything, knows everything, and is in complete control of everything. Nothing is too difficult for him. His character is impeccable; his integrity unquestionable. When God makes a promise, he keeps it. And best of all, his love for you is infinite. He loves you more than you can ever imagine.

Jesus gives us this insight about our heavenly Father, "So if you sinful people know how to give good gifts to your children, how much more will your heavenly Father give good gifts to those who ask him" (Matthew 7:11).

By asking God to be your Matchmaker, you have given him permission to guide you on a supernatural journey that will lead to his best for you, not just in your desire for a soul mate, but in all aspects of your life as well.

> *"Are you serious about wanting God's guidance to become a personal reality in your life? The first step is to tell God that you know you can't manage your own life; that you need his help. "*
> — Catherine Marshall

Think about the matchmaker responsibilities we discussed in the introduction. There is no one who cares more about you than God. He wants to be involved in your life. He understands every aspect of who you are. Furthermore, he knows the person who can best be your soul mate. After all, he created you both. He knows your desires and everything about your current situation. He is able to do whatever is necessary to bring you together at exactly the right time by creating his unique circumstances. And once he does, he will guide you both in the discovery process so you recognize this as his plan for you.

Nicole and I laugh at all of our initial missteps when God first introduced us to each other. And we marvel at how he was able to keep us communicating long enough to see his finger-prints on our relationship.

You have chosen the best possible Matchmaker. Place your life and future into his very capable hands. Enjoy your journey with the Matchmaker—it will be supernatural!

Questions from the Matchmaker

I want to partner with you on your journey but it is your choice. Open up your life to me and you will more fully experience my presence and loving care as I guide you.

1. As you search for a soul mate, what is the main reason you are seeking my help?

2. How would you hope to see our relationship change as we go on this journey together?

3. How can I help you to find your ideal soul mate?

Affirmation

Almighty God, I choose to walk with you by faith on this super-natural journey so you can unveil your ideal plan for me.

THE SECOND TIME AROUND

After you have worked through this devotional series the first time, go through the series again.

1. As you reflect on this devotion for a second time, do you have any new insights?

2. In what ways would you answer the Matchmaker's questions differently at this point in your life?

3. What has changed/is changing in you and your circumstances?

DAY 2
YOU ARE SO LOVED!

See how very much our Father loves us, for he calls us his children,
and that is what we are! But the people who belong to this world don't
recognize that we are God's children because they don't know him.

1 John 3:1

Have you ever thought about why love is so important? People everywhere want to be loved.

God created you in his image, and the very essence of that image is Love. Every person experiences the desire to be loved. But without God's love in us, we feel empty. It is a foundational need for every human being.

We were created to love and be loved. We often seek to fill that need for love through human relationships. But only God can fully satisfy this craving of our heart. Our love relationship with him must be cultivated so this need for security, significance and belonging is satisfied. Then we don't expect someone imperfect to fully fill this vacuum in our heart. There is plenty of space for both relationships, but a relationship without God's love to accompany it, will always leave us feeling as if something is missing.

Perhaps you do not feel worthy of being loved because of something you have done in the past or because of the kind of person you are. The good news is that God loves you and wants a love relationship with you anyway. His love permeates his

"My prayer for you today is that you will feel the loving arms of God wrapped around you."

—Billy Graham

entire being. No person will ever love you more, be as committed to you, or make a greater sacrifice for you than God.

When you experience God's incredible love for you, your need for love is met. You can always rest in his love regardless of your circumstances. Human love, because it is imperfect, will at times fail you, but God's love is solid and unfailing; it will last forever.

God's Love is Unconditional

God loves you because of who he is, not because of what you have done or not done.

> But God demonstrates his own love toward us, in that while we were still sinners, Christ died for us.
> —Romans 5:8, NKJV

God's Love is Unstoppable

No matter what circumstance you find yourself in, you can never be separated from the love God has for you.

> For I am persuaded that neither death nor life, nor angels nor principalities nor powers, nor things present nor things to come, nor height nor depth, nor any other created thing, shall be able to separate us from the love of God which is in Christ Jesus our Lord.
> —Romans 8:38–39, NKJV

God's Love is Unfathomable

God's love for you is so vast that it surpasses anything your mind can even imagine.

> And may you have the power to understand, as all God's people should, how wide, how long, how high, and how

deep his love is. May you experience the love of Christ, though it is too great to understand fully.

—Ephesians 3:18–19

Nurture your love relationship with God and experience his limitless, transforming love for you. Delight in his love and let it become your constant source of assurance in all you do.

Questions from the Matchmaker

Beloved, do you know I love you unconditionally? I ask you to invite me into your daily life so that my love may flow abundantly to you and through you.

1. I love you because of who I am, not because of what you have or haven't done. How does that make you feel?

2. What perceptions do you have about me that are changed by this truth?

3. In what ways are you currently experiencing my love? In what areas of your life will you now accept my love?

Affirmation

Heavenly Father, I embrace your unconditional, unstoppable, unfathomable love for me as I am blessed by your goodness towards me everyday.

THE SECOND TIME AROUND

After you have worked through this devotional series the first time, go through the series again.

1. As you reflect on this devotion for a second time, how are you experiencing God's love in new or different ways?

2. In what ways have you been transformed by the Matchmaker since reading this devotion the first time?

3. In what ways do you see the Matchmaker working in your circumstances?

DAY 3
SOVEREIGNLY UNIQUE

*For we are God's masterpiece. He has created us anew in Christ Jesus,
so we can do the good things he planned for us long ago.*
Ephesians 2:10

Have you ever wondered why you were born now and not 500 or 1000 years ago? Why did God place you into a particular family, culture and country?

God created you for this particular time and place so you would have all the right traits, experiences, and relationships to accomplish the purpose he has for you. Despite how you may feel about where you are in life right now, he has great plans for you. Plans for which he uniquely designed you. Plans that may or may not include marriage. But if marriage is a part of God's plan for your life, he knows the ideal soul mate who will help you accomplish his purposes.

It is important to understand that while God loves you more than you can ever imagine and is committed to your well being as seen from his perspective, you are meant to fulfill part of his master plan. God does not exist to fulfill our plans; we exist to fulfill his.

The journey to fulfill that purpose can be done in fear and anxiousness if we choose to go it alone, or with confidence and peace when we trust in him to take care of the circumstances of life. This may seem harsh but it is critical you understand that

God is God and you are not.

The prophet Isaiah explained it like this, "O LORD, you are our Father. We are the clay, and you are the potter. We all are formed by your hand" (Isaiah 64:8).

You were created to do the good things that God planned for you before you were even born. Your life has purpose. Your life matters. You are significant.

> *"Our Lord never asks us to decide for him; he asks us to yield to him—a very different matter.* "
> — Oswald Chambers

Perhaps you are thinking, "Yeah, God may have had a plan for me but I have royally messed that up by the mistakes I've made." Yes, you may have made mistakes, but that doesn't disqualify you from still fulfilling God's purposes. Through his foreknowledge and sovereignty, his plan for you incorporates your mistakes. Think about Paul's life before he met Jesus on the road to Damascus. He was transformed from a persecutor of Christians into the greatest evangelist of his time. Romans 8:28 promises, "And we know that God causes everything to work together for the good of those who love God and are called according to his purpose for them."

So, what is God's plan for your life? How can you cooperate with him to accomplish what he desires?

God's plan for our lives is usually revealed progressively, one situation at a time. Obviously, most of us would like to see the entire road map now, but that is not how God operates. He wants us to walk by faith, taking one step at a time in the direction he is guiding us. Doing that without fear requires a close relationship with him that involves communication and trust.

God is the creator and we are the created. Each one of us is "God's masterpiece," custom-designed by him to fulfill his purposes. Our ultimate significance is determined by how well we fulfill the plans our creator has for us.

Questions from the Matchmaker

1. How does the perception you now have change when you realize I created you to fulfill my special plans?

2. In what way does knowing that I designed you with a specific plan for your life impact your thoughts and feelings about your future?

3. What am I accomplishing in your life right now because you are single?

Affirmation

Father, help me to learn to hear your voice, and help me to feel the peace and power that come from trusting your plans for me.

THE SECOND TIME AROUND

After you have worked through this devotional series the first time, go through the series again.

1. As you reflect on this devotion for a second time, do you have any new insights?

2. In what ways do currently see the Matchmaker working in and through your life?

3. How do you see God's sovereignty affecting your life circumstances?

DAY 4
IT'S NOT IMPOSSIBLE!

What is impossible for people is possible with God.
Luke 18:27, NIV

Have you sometimes felt like you will never find that special someone with whom to spend the rest of your life? Have obstacles seemed overwhelming? How will you ever find that right person? How will the right person ever find you? Is God really directing you to your soul mate?

Can you relate to any of the following statements as being your barrier to believing God for the impossible?

"Been there, didn't happen."

In the past, you believed God would do something you really wanted—but he never did. So now, if you don't ask God for help, you won't be disappointed when nothing seems to be happening.

"Why do that for me?"

You feel unworthy. Maybe it is guilt about past actions. Or maybe you just don't feel you are good enough now to deserve someone really good.

"I just don't see how."

What's the point in hoping for something when you can't even imagine how it could happen? You don't have the necessary resources or opportunities. Hoping is just wishful thinking.

Each of these barriers result from our misconceptions about God and how he views us. In reality, our heavenly Father, like any parent with greater foresight than the child, says "yes" to requests that will benefit us and "no" to those that are harmful. He is more than able to do anything we can ask. And yes, we are unworthy of his help. But our relationship with God is not based on our performance but rather on his loving and gracious nature. He enjoys giving us good gifts. And he receives the glory and praise when he does something that is far beyond anything we could have predicted based on our knowledge and available resources.

> "We have a God who delights in impossibilites."
> —Andrew Murray

Our Matchmaker is a God who specializes in doing the impossible for his children's good and he wants us to marvel as we watch him work in our lives.

God can do anything and he has limitless abilities. Because he is present everywhere, he sees everything and can intervene anywhere. Because he is all knowing, he has all the facts to make right choices. And because he is all powerful, he has the ability to accomplish whatever is necessary.

Think about that: he is ever-present, all-knowing, and all-powerful. Those infinite abilities make it possible for God to be sovereign—in complete control of everything.

Fortunately, all those abilities reside within our God who is holy—and that means what he does will always be right and just. What he says is true and what he promises will be done.

Can you imagine how awful life would be if God did not have a perfect character and the integrity to guide him in how he sovereignly involves himself in our lives?

The best news of all is that this amazing God cares about you. He is merciful and forgiving when you offend him. He is faithful to always look out for you and your best interests even though you might not be aware what that looks like. He is totally committed to your ultimate happiness and well-being. And he never changes!

The bottom line? With this Matchmaker on your side, nothing is impossible!

QUESTIONS FROM THE MATCHMAKER

1. What do you see as the major obstacles in finding your soul mate?

2. As you consider those obstacles individually, how might I overcome each one on your behalf?

3. Based on your limited understanding and my infinite wisdom and abilities, how would you react if I brought you your soul mate in a way you might have never imagined?

AFFIRMATION

Almighty God, I trust you to do the impossible regardless of my limited understanding, ability, and resources.

THE SECOND TIME AROUND

After you have worked through this devotional series the first time, go through the series again.

1. As you reflect on this devotion for a second time, what has changed for you since your first reading and reflection?

2. In what ways are your answers to the Matchmaker's questions different than before?

3. What has changed in you and your circumstances?

DAY 5
TRUSTING THE MATCHMAKER

Trust in the LORD with all your heart;
do not depend on your own understanding.
Seek his will in all you do, and he will show you which path to take.
Proverbs 3:5–6

How many times as a child did you hope for something impossible? No matter how improbable, you were absolutely convinced that what seemed impossible would happen. But now as an adult you are probably much more guarded about what you hope for.

I (Brad) remember a time when I felt I would never be married again. Why? Because during the years when I was searching for my soul mate, God showed me specific criteria necessary in order for her to be a good fit, given my rather unique lifestyle and circumstances. After thinking about what God had showed me, I came to the conclusion it would be impossible for there to be such a woman. So, I would either have to compromise what God had revealed to me and consequently live to regret it, or I would never be married again.

But God was not limited by my doubts, rather he allowed me to be in unbelief so that when he brought Nicole into my life, I would be amazed at his incredible love for me! I could have been partnering with God in that journey if I had walked by faith, but my lack of trust in no way stopped him from accomplishing what he was going to do. God is pleased when we trust

> "Trustfulness is based on confidence in God whose ways I do not understand."
> —Oswald Chambers

him and live our lives relying on his faithfulness. But that is a process that develops over time as our knowledge of him increases and we repeatedly experience his loving care. However, it is not without struggle. Our human nature is constantly urging us to depend on what we can see, touch, and feel. Meanwhile the Spirit encourages us to believe what God has told us and act accordingly.

The apostle Paul instructs us to "live by faith, not by sight" (2 Corinthians 5:7, NIV). But what does that really mean?

When I received Christ as my Savior and Lord, it was through an act of spiritual faith. I heard the gospel, responded to God's invitation for salvation, believed it to be true, and then, through an act of my will, reached out to God to accept his offer, even though it was not discernible by my five senses.

Colossians 2:6 tells us "So then, just as you received Christ Jesus as Lord, continue to live your lives in him" (NIV).

Continuing to live our lives in him means trusting in him and his character. Because he is trustworthy, we are to believe what he reveals to us with confidence. Then we can follow through on our trust in God and our belief in his word, by taking the appropriate action. As we persevere in doing what God has told us, we will see the fulfillment of what he has promised.

Maybe you are at a point in your journey where you feel it is very unlikely you will ever find your soul mate. Perhaps you have a string of disappointments in your past. With your natural sight, the situation may seem hopeless. But put on your spiritual glasses. Look at the amazing abilities of your Matchmaker and how much he loves you. Then choose to trust him for the impossible.

Questions from the Matchmaker

1. Can you remember a time when you trusted me for something and I was instrumental in making it happen?

2. Can you remember a time when you trusted me for something and it did not happen?

3. Because I am trustworthy, can you think of reasons why I might delay or not give you want you want?

Affirmation

Faithful Father, I choose to trust you for what seems impossible, even though I can't see how it will be accomplished.

THE SECOND TIME AROUND

After you have worked through this devotional series the first time, go through the series again.

1. As you read through this devotion a second time, did you have any new insights?

2. How has your trust in God changed since you first read through this devotion?

3. What are you learning in your daily life about what it means to trust God in all things?

DAY 6
INTIMACY WITH THE MATCHMAKER

Take delight in the LORD, and he will give you your heart's desires.
Psalm 37:4

How would you describe your relationship with God? Formal, superficial, business-like, reciprocal, one-sided, casual, distant, intimate? The good news is that you can have an intimate relationship with God. Intimacy by definition is closeness, and developing an intimate relationship with God requires several ingredients.

First, intimacy involves *desire*. God wants to be desired. Here is how King David expressed his desire for God: "As the deer longs for streams of water, so I long for you, O God. I thirst for God, the living God. When can I go and stand before him?" (Psalm 42:1–2).

Second, intimacy involves *pursuit*. God wants to be pursued. He will even create circumstances in our lives to motivate us to seek him. God promised the prophet Jeremiah, "You will seek me and find me when you seek me with all your heart" (Jeremiah 29:13, NIV).

Anything worth pursuing requires focused attention. And your focus can be measured by the time, energy, and/or money you are willing to invest in your pursuit of God.

Third, intimacy involves *observation*. When you're in love with someone, you enjoy finding out everything you can about the other person. Is that your experience with God? What are his character traits? What's important to him? What pleases him?

God is invisible, but his daily involvement in our lives and

> "*Man was created by God to know and love him in a permanent, personal relationship.*"
>
> —Anne Graham Lotz

presence is obvious to an aware observer. How has he recently demonstrated his love and goodness to you? Do you notice him controlling circumstances? Did he make you aware of his presence during a difficult situation or protect you from harm? What are you learning about him through his Word?

Fourth, intimacy involves *transparency*. You might be thinking, "Why is it necessary for me to be transparent with God if he already knows everything about me?" Being open and honest with God isn't for his benefit, it is for yours.

To a degree we all live pretend lives. We want others to see our strengths and best qualities and we hide the rest. But when we do that we are not really being ourselves. Intimacy requires two people being open about their feelings and allowing their blemishes and imperfections to be seen.

Obviously God doesn't have imperfections and has revealed his true nature to us in the Bible and through his deeds. But he wants us to be vulnerable with him. As we talk with him about our failures, frustrations and fears, our openness establishes a deeper bond with him.

King David wanted to be completely transparent before God. He wrote, "Search me, O God, and know my heart; test me and know my anxious thoughts. Point out anything in me that offends you, and lead me along the path of everlasting life" (Psalm 139:23–24).

True intimacy grows. It isn't instantaneous but develops

and deepens over time. There are no shortcuts. Intimacy is a life-long discovery process that God wants us to have with him. Ask the Holy Spirit to help you be more aware of God's presence throughout your day as you share your thoughts and feelings with him and see his involvement in your life.

QUESTIONS FROM THE MATCHMAKER

1. Honestly, how much desire do you have to pursue greater intimacy with me? What is one step you can take to develop greater intimacy with me?

2. In what ways do you see evidence of my involvement in your daily life?

3. What deep and personal things are you willing to discuss with me? What are you currently withholding from me?

AFFIRMATION

Loving Father, I will pursue a deeper relationship with you by reading your words in the Bible, watching for signs of your goodness, and living with a more conscious awareness of your loving presence.

THE SECOND TIME AROUND

After you have worked through this devotional series the first time, go through the series again.

1. As you reflect on this devotion for a second time, in what ways is your desire for a more imitimate relationship with God growing?

2. In what ways are you actually experiencing greater intimacy with God?

3. What kinds of things keep you from growing deeper in your intimacy with God?

DAY 7
THE MATCHMAKER KNOWS BEST

Whatever is good and perfect is a gift coming down
to us from God our Father.
James 1:17

Given a choice between good and best, almost everyone would choose best. But what is "best"? According to society, best is whatever helps me the most quickly in my current situation. It produces favorable circumstances and accomplishes what I desire. However, according to God, best is whatever helps me the most, not just for this moment in time, but forever. It produces favorable character and accomplishes God's purposes.

Best is not the same for you as it is for me. It is not a universal one-size fits all package. Best is custom-designed by God.

Even though Nicole and I have been married for many years, I continue to marvel at how perfectly she fits me and my many unique needs. She was custom-designed for me! Here are three questions that I found extremely helpful when we were dating as I tried to ascertain God's best for my choice of a soul mate.

Will this choice fit into God's purpose for my life?

God created each one of us for a purpose and anything that interferes with that purpose will distract us.

Many are the plans in a person's heart, but it is the
LORD's purpose that prevails.

—Proverbs 19:21, NIV

It is important to stay focused on God's plans and purposes
and not our own.

Will this choice align with God's guidelines for life?

God created the universe and established the laws and principles
for harmonious life. When we choose to live contrary to those
rules, we will encounter unavoidable problems.

Be careful to obey all my commands, so that all will go
well with you and your children after you, because you
will be doing what is good and pleasing to the LORD
your God.

—Deuteronomy 12:28

God's rules for life are like guideposts or guardrails. They
keep us on the path to his best.

Will this choice pass the test of time?

Best is always determined by time. What is best right now may
look very different a year from now or ten years from now.
Circumstances change and so do people.

Only I can tell you the future before it even happens.
Everything I plan will come to pass, for I do whatever I
wish.

—Isaiah 46:10

Our faithful God's timeframe for life is like a scoreboard
clock that we can't see. No matter what the score may be right
now, best is not obvious until the buzzer sounds and the game
of life is over. God always sees long-range and guides us within
that framework.

The bottom line? Only God can know what's ultimately best. The purpose for our life is clearly understood by him. Your timeframe for life is completely visible to him. Only God is capable of orchestrating the countless variables of life into a journey that leads to his best for you now and into eternity.

"Waiting is the hardest kind of work, but God knows best, and we may joyfully leave all in his hands."

—Lottie Moon

QUESTIONS FROM THE MATCHMAKER

1. Can you remember a time when you were initially attracted to something that looked really good, but with the passing of time it wasn't all that you had hoped it would be?

2. When have you recognized that someone was pursuing a course that wouldn't have a good outcome? Why wouldn't it have been good?

3. Why am I more able to find a perfect soul mate for you than if you were to pursue one on your own?

AFFIRMATION

Father God, I know that you are at work to create the ultimate best for me.

THE SECOND TIME AROUND

After you have worked through this devotional series the first time, go through the series again.

1. What have you learned about making choices since you first read through this devotion?

2. In what ways do your answers to the Matchmaker's questions now differ from when you read this devotion the first time?

3. In what ways are you currently pursuing God's best?

DAY 8
RIGHT ON SCHEDULE

There is a time for everything,
and a season for every activity under the heavens.
Ecclesiastes 3:1, NIV

We live in a culture that demands instant gratification. We want what we want and we want it now! But God is never in a hurry.

The prophet Jeremiah wrote, "The LORD is good to those whose hope is in him, to the one who seeks him; it is good to wait quietly for the salvation of the LORD" (Lamentations 3:25–26, NIV). Is your hope centered in God as you patiently wait for him to rescue you from your current situation?

Waiting is difficult, especially when we see others taking shortcuts to achieve what we desire. But King David reminds us to, "Be still before the LORD and wait patiently for him; do not fret when people succeed in their ways, when they carry out their wicked schemes" (Psalm 37:7, NIV).

When we get what we want prematurely, we shortchange ourselves. It may not be apparent right away, but time always reveals the consequences of impatience.

I (Brad) remember many Christmases and birthdays when I prayed for God's special gift of a soul mate. Those events came and went without my prayer being answered. Why? Because with more time, Nichole and I would be more ideally suited for each other. More time was needed to change our situations so our life circumstances would be a better fit.

God is in complete control of everything. Any delays are not because he isn't able to make things happen faster. Rather, he has more he wants to accomplish in us and through us during a slower, more deliberate journey to the ultimate destination.

God sees everything that concerns us and has a complete view of our future. With our limited foresight, we can only base our judgments and decisions on what we know presently. Our assumptions about the future are only our best guesses. But God knows about the major changes that are coming around the next bend.

"You have a time-table, and God has a timetable. His is better than yours."

—Criswell Freeman

Our faithful and loving God is more committed to our long-term happiness and well-being than to our immediate pleas for what we want right now. Because of our impatience, all too often we are willing to settle for something or someone that we know is less than ideal. But when we have accepted God as our matchmaker, he steps in and stops us from trading away the far better future he has planned for us.

In my search for a soul mate, I met several wonderful Christian ladies during my dating journey. But something always brought the relationship to an end. And each time I experienced great heartbreak and disappointment. Why was this happening? I was praying and asking God for his help. I believed each one of those ladies was the best I could hope for. But God knew better. He knew Nicole was in my future and he was not going to let me marry someone else.

To be impatient with God's timing is to question his ability, goodness and love for us. Psalm 27:14 tells us, "Wait patiently for the LORD. Be brave and courageous. Yes, wait patiently for the LORD." Best is always worth the wait.

QUESTIONS FROM THE MATCHMAKER

1. Think about a time when you desperately wanted some thing to happen and it didn't. Then later you were relieved because I gave you more insight.

2. What makes it hard for you right now to be patient in waiting to discover your soul mate?

3. What might be some reasons that I have for not revealing a soul mate to you right now?

AFFIRMATION

Sovereign God, I trust in the perfectness of your timing even though it is hard for me to wait.

THE SECOND TIME AROUND

After you have worked through this devotional series the first time, go through the series again.

1. As you reflect on this devotion for a second time, do you have any new insights?

2. What are you learning about God's timing?

3. What has changed in you and your circumstances since the first time you read through this devotion?

DAY 9
TALKING WITH THE MATCHMAKER

Don't worry about anything; instead, pray about everything.
Tell God what you need, and thank him for all he has done.
Philippians 4:6

Are you used to going it alone? Do you think it is up to you to solve your own problems?

That's not what God wants. He is there for you. But you need to talk with him about what is going on in your life. As a Christian, you do this through prayer.

Prayer is taking time to talk with your heavenly Father, the one you have asked to be your Matchmaker. It is a conversation where you can share what's on your heart and anticipate God's response. Prayer is a vital part of developing your relationship with God.

God wants you to seek his guidance, comfort, peace, and intimate companionship at all times … not just when you want something. He has the answers to all of life's questions!

When you are praying, God is listening … and he will answer—if not immediately then eventually.

So why does God want you to spend time talking with him?

God wants to develop a relationship with you.

Come near to God and he will come near to you.

—James 4:8, NIV

God wants to bless you.

So if you sinful people know how to give good gifts to your children, how much more will your heavenly Father give good gifts to those who ask him.

—Matthew 7:11

God wants to meet your needs.

Let us then approach God's throne of grace with confidence, so that we may receive mercy and find grace to help us in our time of need.

—Hebrews 4:16, NIV

Talk with the Matchmaker about your life and your desire for a soul mate. Openly share your thoughts and feelings. Invite him to open your mind and heart to embrace what he has for you. Then listen for his prompting through the Holy Spirit, seek his insights within the Bible, and watch for his orchestration of your circumstances.

> *"God's help is always available, but it is only given to those who seek it."*
>
> —Max Lucado

As you learn more about the faithfulness of God, the more you will trust him; and the more you trust him, the more you will enjoy talking with him. Because God is your perfect heavenly Father, you can pray with confidence knowing that he is listening and will answer your prayers!

Keep the communication lines open. You are on an exciting journey with the Matchmaker.

QUESTIONS FROM THE MATCHMAKER

1. What thoughts do you have about just "being" with me during times of prayer?

2. How does it make you feel to know I want to spend time with you and listen to what's important to you?

3. What guidance are you seeking right now?

AFFIRMATION

Heavenly Father, I will talk with you about everything because I know you hear me.

THE SECOND TIME AROUND

After you have worked through this devotional series the first time, go through the series again.

1. In what ways have your interactions with God changed since the first time you read through this devotion?

2. Would you answer any of the Matchmaker's questions differently than you did the first time?

3. In what ways is your relationship with your heavenly Father changing?

DAY 10
DOING SOMETHING NEW

See, I am doing a new thing! Now it springs up; do you not perceive it?
I am making a way in the wilderness and streams in the wasteland.
Isaiah 43:19, NIV

You've probably heard it said that the definition of lunacy is doing the same thing over and over again but expecting a different result. And yet, as creatures of habit, we tend to not want to try new ways of doing things.

As I (Brad) look back over my life, there have been numerous major events that were horrible at the time. But after each one, God brought me to a new place in life that was much better than the one before. And yet, each time I fought to hang on to the present because I had no idea how much better the "new" around the next corner of life would be.

God is constantly bringing about something new in our lives. The most dramatic change occurred when we invited Christ into our lives and were born again into God's forever family.

> Therefore, if anyone is in Christ, the new creation has come: the old has gone, the new has come!
> —2 Corinthians 5:17, NIV

God uses change to transform us so our character will reflect the qualities that Jesus demonstrated when he walked on earth.

Consider it pure joy, my brothers and sisters, whenever you face trials of many kinds, because you know that the testing of your faith produces perseverance. Let perseverance finish its work so that you may be mature and complete, not lacking anything.

—James 1:2–4, NIV

"The amazing thing about Jesus is that he doesn't just patch up our lives, he gives us a brand-new sheet, a clean slate to start over, all new."

—Gloria Gaither

God uses change to transform our situations because he wants us to accomplish the good things and purposes for which he created us. He designed us with specific abilities. He placed each one of us in a particular family and environment. All so he can accomplish what he has planned for us.

For we are God's masterpiece. He has created us anew in Christ Jesus, so we can do the good things he planned for us long ago.

—Ephesians 2:10

God uses change to transform our relationships because he wants us to experience and share the depth of love that is characteristic of his very nature.

Dear friends, since God so loved us, we also ought to love one another. No one has ever seen God; but if we love one another, God lives in us and his love is made complete in us.

—1 John 4:11–12, NIV

Learn to embrace change. Your life is in the hands of your

heavenly Father who will lead you into a glorious future.

"For I know the plans I have for you," declares the LORD, "plans to prosper you and not to harm you, plans to give you hope and a future."

—Jeremiah 29:11, NIV

God desires the very best for you and he has mapped out a perfect course for your life that will result in your utmost joy and fulfillment. Embrace the change, even though it may be difficult and is moving you beyond your comfort zone. Trust the Matchmaker. He knows what he is doing.

QUESTIONS FROM THE MATCHMAKER

1. What changes are you facing in your life?

2. Based on my commitment to your well-being, what are some of the good things that I may be doing for you as a result of these changes?

3. What do you need to let go of from the past as you trust me and walk with me into a new future?

AFFIRMATION

Sovereign Lord, I am excited to see the new things you are doing and will bring about in my life.

THE SECOND TIME AROUND

After you have worked through this devotional series the first time, go through the series again.

1. Since reading this devotion for the first time, what new things from God have you experienced or received?

2. In what ways are your answers to the Matchmaker's questions different now?

3. What is new or changing in your life?

PART 2

YOUR BELIEFS
ABOUT LIFE

DAY 11
THE NEW YOU

This means that anyone who belongs to Christ has become a new person.
The old life is gone; a new life has begun!
2 Corinthians 5:17

What kind of self-image do you have?

The apostle Paul encouraged the believers in Rome with this statement, "Don't think you are better than you really are. Be honest in your evaluation of yourselves, measuring yourselves by the faith God has given us" (Romans 12:3).

God doesn't want you to have an inferiority complex or a superiority complex. He wants you to see yourself correctly. Who are you really?

There are three perceptions of "you": 1) who you think you are, 2) who others think you are, 3) who God knows you are.

> *"Being born again is God's solution to our need for love and life and light."*
> —Anne Graham Lotz

If you want to experience God's best with a future soul mate then you must learn to see yourself as God sees you. When you do, you will begin to see that the transformation you are experiencing is being guided by the direction of the Holy Spirit.

The "new you" actually came into being the instant you

45

invited Jesus into your life as your Savior and Lord. You were spiritually born again. At that moment God exchanged your old identity for a brand new one.

By receiving Jesus, the following statements are now true:

You are God's child.

But to all who believed him and accepted him, he gave the right to become children of God.

—John 1:12

The same God who has the power to speak the universe into being claims you as his adopted child. He loves you unconditionally and is always available to hear your prayers and help you.

You are a saint with a new nature.

Greet all the saints in Christ Jesus.

—Philippians 4:21, BSB

Each one of us has been given a new righteous nature in Christ. When you focus on your new nature as a saint, you no longer see yourself as a sinner, but as someone righteous in God's eyes who still sins occasionally when deceived by the old nature.

You are a member of God's forever family.

You are the body of Christ, and each one of you is a part of it.

—1 Corinthians 12:27, NIV

God never intended for us to live the Christian life alone. As believers, we are a community of brothers and sisters in Christ who are interdependent. We are a holy family that is to be characterized by love and unity.

You are a citizen of Christ's heavenly kingdom.

Our citizenship is in heaven.

—Philippians 3:20, NIV

Because you haven't physically moved out of the earthly kingdom, it is easy to have confused loyalties. However, you now serve a different king.

By faith, continually accept the reality of who you are in Christ and allow God to help you conform to your new identity. Start believing what God says is true about you. When we establish our identity in how God sees us, we can confidently live in the assurance of his perfect plan for our lives.

QUESTIONS FROM THE MATCHMAKER

1. In what ways does knowing that you are my child and I love you unconditionally change some of your perceptions about yourself?

2. In what ways can you see that the new identity I have given you is influencing your decisions?

3. How does knowing you belong to me, are a member of my forever family and a citizen of heaven, intertwine with your desire for a soul mate?

AFFIRMATION

Father God, I embrace the fact that my past doesn't have to dictate my future because I am a new person in Jesus Christ.

THE SECOND TIME AROUND

After you have worked through this devotional series the first time, go through the series again.

1. As you reflect on this devotion for a second time, do you have any new insights about your nature in Christ?

2. In what ways would you answer any of the Matchmaker's questions differently now?

3. How do you see your new nature in Christ making a difference in your life and your desires for a soul mate?

DAY 12
SEEING IS BELIEVING

Your eye is a lamp that provides light for your body.
When your eye is good, your whole body is filled with light.
But when your eye is bad, your whole body is filled with darkness.
Matthew 6:22–23

How often do you question if what you see and hear is the truth? This is particularly important when it comes to people who want us to trust them. Who can we believe? How can we separate fact from fiction? What is really going on? How can we know our decision-making is based on truth and not simply perception?

It starts with perspective. We all have a natural perspective that is influenced by our core convictions. These convictions have been developed by our education, experiences, and life circumstances. Perspective is the way we look at life. It is our mindset. And it affects all that we assume to be true and important.

> *"What we believe determines how we behave, and both determine what we become."*
> —Warren Wiersbe

However, sometimes we arrive at our conclusions in the midst of an environment that is filled with scams and deception. If our perspective is wrong, we will be taking in falsehoods that we believe are true. And yet with

49

the passing of time the future will reveal the wisdom of our reasoning. Deceptions are always eventually exposed, and the truth prevails.

If we want to experience God's best in life then we must first make sure that our core convictions are consistent with the truth he has revealed to us in his Word.

God wants us to ground our life in his perspective because his view is not limited by anything. He sees it all. Our perspective is limited by what has been presented to us by appearances and surface issues. True perspective is only possible by believing God about what he sees and knows.

John 16:13 tells us, "When he, the Spirit of truth, comes, he will guide you into all truth" (NIV). We are exposed to God's perspective when the Holy Spirit reveals truth to us:
—through God's Word
—through prayer
—through other people
—through circumstances
—through the Holy Spirit's prompting

Truth demands application. We must allow the truth to change us as God desires. To do so, guard against ignoring what God has revealed to you, or minimizing the importance of the truth and rationalizing a way around it.

Ask the Holy Spirit to help you see your life and all its circumstances from God's perspective. When we see God's truth, we can believe and trust his direction. We can make wise decisions, based on beliefs and values that will lead to a future built on a solid foundation.

Questions from the Matchmaker

1. How does "seeing" my truth influence what you can and should "believe"?

2. In what ways are you currently trying to align your view point with mine?

3. Can you think of a time your personal perspective compromised one of your decisions? How might asking for my perspective have changed the outcome?

Affirmation

Heavenly Father, I choose your perspective even when it might be difficult to embrace. I know that you see and know all things and you have my very best interests in mind.

THE SECOND TIME AROUND

After you have worked through this devotional series the first time, go through the series again.

1. How is embracing God's perspective changing what you see and believe?

2. In what ways is your life changing as you seek God's viewpoint through his Word, through prayer, through other people, and through circumstances?

3. In what ways do you see God working in and through your life circumstances?

DAY 13
THE MATCHMAKER'S GUIDEBOOK

Don't copy the behavior and customs of this world,
but let God transform you into a new person
by changing the way you think.
Then you will learn to know God's will for you,
which is good and pleasing and perfect.

Romans 12:2

Jeremiah 29:11 tells us, "I know the plans I have for you," declares the LORD, "plans to prosper you and not to harm you, plans to give you hope and a future" (NIV). God wants us to know him and the plans he has for us. He wants us to discover the great depth of his love for us and commitment for us. The Bible contains his words of love and direction.

God has given us his Word in the Bible and his indwelling Spirit to help us look at life and our current situation from his perspective. The Bible contains the truths that are vital to experiencing God's best in life and eternity. It is God's instruction manual to us for successful and supernatural living. As you read the Bible and pray, the Holy Spirit will bring God's best for you into focus.

> *"The Scriptures were not given for our inform- ation, but for our transformation."*
>
> —D. L. Moody

As Christians, we are disciples of Christ. We should be committed to learning his truth and following his directions. Use the following steps and questions periodically as you pray and seek to apply God's truth in your life.

The Process of Renewing Your Mind
1. *Receptivity*—Check your attitude.
- Do I really believe that God's truth can transform me?
- Am I willing to let God's truth change me and my life?
- Has God already revealed truth to me I am unwilling to obey?
- Am I cultivating a submissive and obedient attitude?

2. *Comprehension*—Check your level of understanding.
- What new truth have I become aware of by reading my Bible, paying attention to the promptings of the Holy Spirit, and going to church or listening to other Christians?
- What does this truth mean with regard to what I think, say, and do?
- What are the consequences of not applying this truth to my life?

3. *Conviction*—Check your level of belief.
- Am I convinced that it is important to apply this new revealed truth to my life as God shows me how?
- Do I truly believe that God is working in and through his Holy Spirit to lead me?

4. Transformation—Check your commitment.
- Am I willing to embrace what God has revealed to me and allow it to change my perception and actions?
- What is the next thing I should do to cooperate with the Holy Spirit in my transformation?

James 1:22 tells us, "Do not merely listen to the Word, and so deceive yourselves. Do what it says." God has given us the Bible to help us in our journey of discovery. Allow the Holy Spirit to use it in your life and enjoy the adventure.

QUESTIONS FROM THE MATCHMAKER

1. In what ways are you currently allowing my Word to mold your life?

2. Which of my promises can you apply to your current circumstances?

3. As you consider a relationship with a soul mate, how important is it to you that that person make my Word a priority in guiding their life?

AFFIRMATION

Father God, you have given me your Word and your Spirit to help me know your will for my life. I want to be transformed by your power working in me.

THE SECOND TIME AROUND

After you have worked through this devotional series the first time, go through the series again.

1. In what ways is God's Word transforming you?

2. What are you learning about God and his will for your life as you read and study his Word?

3. Are there any ways that you see your circumstances changing as you seek to be led by God's Word and the Holy Spirit?

DAY 14
WORTHY OF DEVOTION

You must not have any other god but me.
You must not make for yourself an idol of any kind
or an image of anything in the heavens or on the earth or in the sea.
You must not bow down to them or worship them,
for I, the LORD your God, am a jealous God
who will not tolerate your affection for any other gods.
Exodus 20:3–5

What or who are you most committed to? Is your thought life preoccupied with a particular person or goal?

For many people, idolatry is a foreign concept, something ancient and pagan. But in reality, idolatry is the heart being possessed and more devoted to anything other than God.

> *"You must never sacrifice your relationship with God for the sake of a relationship with another person."*
> —Charles Stanley

For single believers the desire for marriage can become an obsession. Of course, there is nothing wrong with seeking a godly spouse to love, honor, and cherish. A marriage that honors Christ is both holy and beautiful. But at what point do our desires actually become the all-consuming sin of idolatry?

Our creator God knows we

will live our best life when our hearts are wholly devoted to him. We need to learn to make every person and thing less important than our relationship with God. That of course is difficult because our attention and affections are easily captivated by whatever we believe will bring us the happiness we so desire right now. However, the apostle Paul assures us, "The temptations in your life are no different from what others experience. And God is faithful. He will not allow the temptation to be more than you can stand. When you are tempted, he will show you a way out so that you can endure. So, my dear friends, flee from the worship of idols" (1 Corinthians 10:13–14).

Do you need to put things back into the proper biblical alignment? If so, take these three steps:

First, turn back and restore God to his proper place in your life. Pray that he will help you resist the temptation to focus too much of your time and energy on the search for a spouse (or whatever else has become number one in your life). Ask God to fill you with an increased desire for him and for those things that are his priorities.

Second, remember that as Christians we are God's vessels—created to reflect his goodness in all we do, whether married or single. Is your desire for marriage and your quest for a soul mate blocking the Holy Spirit's work in your life?

Finally, remember that before we ever become engaged to an earthly mate, we are already betrothed to the Bridegroom, who is Christ (see Ephesians 5:25–27). Imagine how disrespectful it would be for a bride to walk down the church aisle with her eyes darting around at the flowers or the stained-glass windows, admiring everything but her future spouse. Yet such a tragedy becomes reality when we focus more on our quest for a mate than on a relationship with our heavenly Beloved.

As Christians, the deep hole of loneliness we may feel within while we are single is God-shaped, not ring-shaped. It can only be filled by him, not by a mate, no matter how ideal that mate might be.

QUESTIONS FROM THE MATCHMAKER

1. How much of your mind, your time, and your heart is committed to your search for a soul mate?

2. How does your search for a soul mate make you feel? Anxious? Discouraged? Excited? Hopeful? Are you trusting in my timing?

3. How can I help you to refocus so I am the highest priority in your life?

AFFIRMATION

Heavenly Father, because you have placed such a high priority on developing a relationship with me, I will honor you by placing a high priority on our relationship as well. I want to keep you as first place in my life always.

THE SECOND TIME AROUND

After you have worked through this devotional series the first time, go through the series again.

1. What is your number one priority in life right now?

2. Does your search for a soul mate have its proper place in your life?

3. What is God teaching you about your search for a soul mate?

DAY 15
VOICES IN YOUR HEAD

We demolish arguments and every pretension that sets itself up
against the knowledge of God,
and we take captive every thought to make it obedient to Christ.
2 Corinthians 10:5, NIV

Do you trust your thoughts? Most people do. And almost everyone assumes the thoughts in their head are their own. But in reality, at any given time, the thoughts you assume to be your own can actually originate from four different sources.

Some Thoughts Are from God

God is able to give us divine insights. For example, at one point Jesus asked his disciples who they thought he was. "Simon Peter answered, 'You are the Messiah, the Son of the living God.' Jesus replied, 'You are blessed, Simon son of John, because my Father in heaven has revealed this to you. You did not learn this from any human being'" (Matthew 16:16–17).

Peter spoke what he was thinking without realizing the thought had originated from the Holy Spirit.

Some Thoughts Are from Satan

Later Jesus was explaining that he would need to go to Jerusalem where he would suffer, die, and then be raised from the dead. Peter took issue with what Jesus had just said. "'Heaven forbid, Lord,' he said. 'This will never happen to you!' Jesus turned to Peter and said, 'Get away from me, Satan! You are a dangerous trap to me. You are seeing things merely from a human point of view, not from God's'" (Matthew 16:22–23).

> "We can't stop the Adversary from whispering in our ears, but we can refuse to listen, and we can definitely refuse to respond."
> —Liz Curtis Higgs

Although well-intentioned, Peter had become Satan's spokesperson, and Jesus, recognizing the origin of the thought, rebuked him.

Some Thoughts Are from Our Old Nature

Because we are born as sinful beings, our natural thinking becomes polluted with concepts that are contrary to God. Paul explains it like this, "The mind of the flesh is death, but the mind of the Spirit is life and peace, because the mind of the flesh is hostile to God" (Romans 8:6–7).

This old pattern of thinking is natural to us even after we become followers of Christ. That's why Paul also said, "Don't copy the behavior and customs of this world, but let God transform you into a new person by changing the way you think. Then you will learn to know God's will for you, which is good and pleasing and perfect" (Romans 12:2). God uses the truths and principles found in the Bible to reshape our thinking pattern.

Some Thoughts Are from Our New Nature

As the Holy Spirit renews our mind, we develop a new pattern of thinking. In 1 Corinthians 2:16 we read, "'Who can know the LORD's thoughts? Who knows enough to teach him?' But we understand these things, for we have the mind of Christ."

To think with the mind of Christ means we now view life through this new filter of his values and desires.

The Importance of Right Thinking

In order to identify a thought that is not from God, ask the Holy Spirit for help. He can expose thoughts and attitudes that are contrary to God's will and lead you into all truth (see John 16:13). It's not a sin to have a bad thought enter your mind. It only becomes destructive if you permit it to remain and dwell on it.

"And now, dear brothers and sisters, one final thing. Fix your thoughts on what is true, and honorable, and right, and pure, and lovely, and admirable. Think about things that are excellent and worthy of praise" (Philippians 4:8).

QUESTIONS FROM THE MATCHMAKER

1. What thoughts occupy your thinking throughout a typical day? Which are consistent with God's viewpoint? Which are not?

2. When did thoughts lead you into a bad situation?

3. Why is it important for you to embrace truth instead of deceptive thoughts as you are on this soul mate journey with me?

AFFIRMATION

All-knowing God, I choose to embrace thoughts that are from you and reject those that are in opposition to your values, ways, and purposes.

THE SECOND TIME AROUND

After you have worked through this devotional series the first time, go through the series again.

1. As you reflect on this devotion for a second time, do you have any new insights?

2. In what ways do you see God's truth influencing the way you think?

3. In what ways is God's truth making an impact on your search for a soul mate?

DAY 16
GROWING IN TOUGH TIMES

We can rejoice, too, when we run into problems and trials,
for we know that they help us develop endurance.
And endurance develops strength of character,
and character strengthens our confident hope of salvation.
And this hope will not lead to disappointment.
For we know how dearly God loves us,
because he has given us the Holy Spirit to fill our hearts with his love.
Romans 5:3–5

Each one of us has experienced difficulties at various times throughout our life. Usually these trials dominate a day, or maybe a week. But there are other times when we encounter a crisis that is life altering. When that happens, we find ourselves walking through a valley so dark and deep we wonder if we will ever see sunshine again.

I (Brad) have had several crisis situations during my life. At the time it felt as though these valley experiences would never end. Those were tough times filled with disappointment, doubt, discouragement, and fear.

With every trial, we face the temptation to abandon God while the evil one whispers in our ear "Give up on God. After all, hasn't he abandoned you?" But in reality, God is with us even in our darkest hours, regardless of what our emotions or demonic voices tell us. God knows what we are going through and reaches out his hand, not to save us from the situation but so we can walk through that valley with him.

> "When you go through deep waters, I will be with you. When you go through rivers of difficulty, you will not drown. When you walk through the fire of oppression, you will not be burned up; the flames will not consume you."
>
> —Isaiah 43:2

> *"Our loving God uses difficulty in our lives to burn away the sin of self and build faith and spiritual power."*
> —Bill Bright

Adversity looks a whole lot better when you see it through your rearview mirror. It's only when a crisis is far enough in your past that you can see the bigger picture and appreciate the good that God accomplished through pain and suffering.

God uses adversity as a tool to refine us and increase our capacity for greatness.

> Dear brothers and sisters, when troubles come your way, consider it an opportunity for great joy. For you know that when your faith is tested, your endurance has a chance to grow. So let it grow, for when your endurance is fully developed, you will be perfect and complete, needing nothing.
>
> —James 1:2–4

Perhaps the most difficult crises are the ones where we felt betrayed by those we trusted. God molds us and shapes us through trials. But when he has used others in the process, we can leave the valley shouldering bitterness toward them. As a result, in a sense, we imprison ourselves with unforgiveness.

Difficult life experiences shape us. Through those experiences, God allows us the opportunity to grow in our spiritual character so we reflect more of his values and strength. But it is our choice whether we allow that transformation to take place. If we harbor resentment toward God and others, we will leave the valley diminished instead of stronger.

> And we know that God causes everything to work together for the good of those who love God and are called according to his purpose for them.
> —Romans 8:28

QUESTIONS FROM THE MATCHMAKER

1. Take some time to look at your past difficult experiences through my eyes. What good came out of those tough situations?

2. What are the recent problems or trials in your life for which you are stilling trusting me with the outcome? How can I help you endure?

3. What unresolved bitterness or unforgiveness do I need to help you deal with today so it doesn't affect your tomorrows?

AFFIRMATION

Gracious heavenly Father, I choose to rely on you when the adversities of life press in on me.

THE SECOND TIME AROUND

After you have worked through this devotional series the first time, go through the series again.

1. As you reflect on this devotion for a second time, do you have any new insights?

2. What positive character qualities can you identify in your life that have come as a result of a trial or difficulty that you have experienced?

3. What are you learning about God and about yourself as you journey toward finding a soul mate?

DAY 17
MOVING ON

No, dear brothers and sisters, I have not achieved it,
but I focus on this one thing: Forgetting the past
and looking forward to what lies ahead
Philippians 3:13

Experiences from our past have a strong effect on our lives and our behavior. Great experiences can give us confidence and faith. However, sometimes tough experiences can make us bitter, fearful, and untrusting which can produce a devastating effect on our lives and our relationships.

Most of us have some history we would like to erase. How about you? Are you haunted by things you did—things you want to forget, actions for which you still feel condemned?

Before the apostle Paul became a committed disciple of Christ, he was a persecutor of the followers of Jesus. This was part of his history that he wished he could erase. And even after he became a Christian, he still struggled with his old nature and at times slipped into sin. Paul shares his struggle and Christ's solution,

> Oh, what a miserable person I am! Who will free me from this life that is dominated by sin and death? Thank God! The answer is in Jesus Christ our Lord. So you see

how it is: In my mind I really want to obey God's law, but because of my sinful nature I am a slave to sin.

—Romans 7:24–25

He continues,

So now there is no condemnation for those who belong to Christ Jesus. And because you belong to him, the power of the life-giving Spirit has freed you from the power of sin that leads to death.

—Romans 8:1–2

We need to see beyond the sins and mistakes of yesterday so we can embrace Christ's promises for tomorrow. Today, accept the grace and forgiveness Christ has provided to us so we can be free to live the new life he has planned for us.

John, the apostle, explains it like this, "If we confess our sins, he is faithful and just and will forgive us our sins and purify us from all unrighteousness" (1 John 1:9, NIV). We can't earn God's forgiveness. It is freely given by him when we acknowledge we have worked against him and ask him for forgiveness. Then he will remove "our sins as far from us as the east is from the west" (Psalm 103:12).

> *"Trust the past to God's mercy, the present to God's love, and the future to God's providence."*
>
> —Saint Augustine

God has an overall plan that is not thwarted by anyone's mistakes. Negative experiences will be turned into positives for our future when we let God heal us and teach us what we can learn from them—allowing him to conform us to the image of Christ.

QUESTIONS FROM THE MATCHMAKER

1. I don't want you to be weighed down by guilt and condemnation from your past. Look deep, what is still taking a toll on you? Give it to me.

2. What guilt can you share with me? It is my desire that once you have experienced my forgiveness in this matter, you may be able to forgive yourself as well.

3. Think about your past and my abundant forgiveness. How does this affect your view of the future?

AFFIRMATION

Gracious God, I will focus on the possibilities of the present and not be guilt-ridden by habits or mistakes I have made in the past. I entrust my future into your hands.

THE SECOND TIME AROUND

After you have worked through this devotional series the first time, go through the series again.

1. In what ways are you currently moving on from your past?

2. In what ways have you experienced God's healing and grace in regard to past mistakes and sin?

3. When it comes to your past, what do you still need to entrust into God's loving hands?

DAY 18
PROMISES MADE, PROMISES KEPT

But Ruth replied, "Don't urge me to leave you or to turn back from you.
Where you go I will go, and where you stay I will stay.
Your people will be my people and your God my God."
Ruth 1:16, NIV

L ife is filled with commitments. Every person lives within a cluster of commitments that have accumulated over their lifetime. Some represent responsibilities or promises while others are simply personal preferences. These obligations and attachments greatly affect what a person brings into a relationship and what will need to be factored into your relationship when making future decisions.

What are your current commitments? What new commitments do you anticipate in your future? How do these commitments blend with the commitments your potential mate has? Children from a previous marriage? Elderly parents requiring care? Vocational commitments? Financial commitments? Are you willing to accept those attachments and is the person you are dating willing to accept yours?

Promises are easy to make and sometimes difficult to fulfill. What do you do when commitments clash or get in the way of something new you desire?

The book of Ruth has an excellent example of the kind of commitment that God blesses. Ruth lived in Moab. Her mother-in-law, Naomi, had moved away from Israel to Moab with her husband and sons during a time of great famine in Judah. Ruth had married one of Naomi's sons.

But when Naomi's husband and two sons die, she sees her only chance at survival is to return to her homeland in Judea. She encourages her daughters-in-law to go home to their own families. But Ruth was committed to her mother-in-law.

> *"Integrity is keeping a commitment even after circumstances have changed."*
>
> —David Jeremiah

Ruth leads a pauper's life while caring for Naomi in her new homeland. She gathers grain dropped by the gleaners during harvest just so they can have food to eat. Her commitment was seen by a land owner, Boaz, who was impressed by her faithfulness in spite of hardship. Through a series of events orchestrated by God, Ruth marries Boaz. Not only does Ruth's physical existence go from rags to riches, but in that unexpected union, Ruth bears a son who becomes the grandfather of King David and an ancestor of Jesus Christ!

Because faithfulness is one of God's attributes, he rewards us when we honor commitments we have made. Galatians 6:9 reminds us, "Let us not become weary in doing good, for at the proper time we will reap a harvest if we do not give up" (NIV).

Sometimes our commitments feel like a burden when our situation has changed. We made commitments with one set of circumstances but then as life moves forward, we're left with the wish we'd never made such a commitment. God uses this opportunity to increase in us the attribute of faithfulness.

Changing circumstances in our lives might surprise us, but never God. We honor him when we honor those to whom we've made a commitment. Are you cultivating or destroying your ability to keep commitments? How about the person you are dating or looking forward to date? When you marry, former commitments should be accepted as part of the union. Marriage represents one of the most important commitments a person can make. How past commitments are handled is an indication of how they will be dealt with in the future.

Questions from the Matchmaker

1. What commitments have you made that became or have become difficult to keep because circumstances changed?

2. In what ways have I blessed you because you honored a difficult commitment?

3. I know the current commitments you have; what type of soul mate would fit into those commitments?

Affirmation

Faithful God, with your help, I will honor the commitments I have, even when they are not convenient or require sacrifice.

THE SECOND TIME AROUND

After you have worked through this devotional series the first time, go through the series again.

1. In what ways are your commitments impacting your search for a soul mate?

2. In what ways does honoring the commitments that you have in your life also honor God?

3. In what ways do you see God working in and through your commitments?

DAY 19
MADE JUST RIGHT

I praise you because I am fearfully and wonderfully made;
your works are wonderful, I know that full well.
Psalm 139:14, NIV

You've probably heard it said, "Beauty is in the eye of the beholder." So how beautiful are you? Well, that depends on who's looking at you.

When you look at yourself, you're usually comparing yourself with others who you think are attractive, talented, or popular. And you wish you could be more like them.

When others look at you, they have their own standards for what they are looking for. Those ideals are shaped by their peer group, media influences, and social norms.

When God looks at you, how does he see you? If you are a believer, he sees you as perfect. Why? Because of all that Jesus Christ accomplished in his death and resurrection. God sees your life embodied in his Son.

The reality is, you are special; God custom-designed you. God told the prophet Jeremiah, "Before I formed you in the womb I knew you, before you were born I set you apart" (Jeremiah 1:5). Job acknowledged that he was the result of God's handiwork, "Your hands shaped me and made me" (Job 10:8). King David praised God as he considered how he was designed by his creator: "For you created my inmost being, you knit me together in my mother's womb. I praise you because I am fearfully and wonderfully made; your works are wonderful" (Psalm 139:13–14, NIV).

What about the things that you have always disliked about how you were designed? Are those things defects or did God intentionally make you that way for a reason?

Our all-powerful, all-wise, and all-loving heavenly Father personally shaped you. And he set you apart for a special purpose while you were still in your mother's womb.

> "*God doesn't make junk.*"
> —Ethel Waters

Many people do not acknowledge that they have been made by the hand of God. They believe that they are merely the product of chance—a human grab bag containing 23,000 genes. And if there was no special design then there are no expectations as to what their life should accomplish. But the truth is, God has custom-designed each one of us.

We are born with different personalities. These personal qualities affect how we think, what we value, and what we do. For example, some people are extrovert while others are introvert. Some like adventure and variety while others prefer stability and routine. There are many traits that are blended into various personality combinations. While you were still in your mother's womb, God designed a personality for you that is perfectly suited for his plan for you.

Different people have different abilities. These natural skills enable us to do certain things well. Some people are athletic, some are musical, some are artistic, and some are mechanical. The abilities that you have were not randomly assigned to you. God has given you specific abilities so you can better serve him and his kingdom.

Don't allow the labels or perceptions of others to define you. God has wonderfully designed you. And when the Matchmaker introduces you to your soul mate, they will see you as ideal for them because they too were custom-designed by God to fit you perfectly.

QUESTIONS FROM THE MATCHMAKER

1. How does it make you feel to know that I, the creator of the universe, have custom-made you?

2. What are some of the unique qualities and talents that you possess because of my special design of you?

3. In what ways are you serving me with your specific mix of custom-designed qualities?

AFFIRMATION

Creator God, I am a beautiful person because you made me!

THE SECOND TIME AROUND

After you have worked through this devotional series the first time, go through the series again.

1. Do you tend to focus on how you see yourself, how others see you, or how God sees you? What impact does this perspective have on you and the things in life that you are experiencing?

2. Having read through this devotion a second time, would you answer any of the Matchmaker's questions differently now?

3. What are you learning about your specific God-given talents?

DAY 20
FREELY GIVEN

From his abundance
we have all received one gracious blessing after another.
John 1:16

Have you ever been around someone who made you feel like you just didn't measure up to their expectations? No matter what you did, it never seemed quite good enough?

In reality, we don't measure up to God's standard either. We aren't good enough. That is why Jesus died on the cross for our sin and has clothed us with his righteousness. God bestows his goodness on us, not because we are worthy, but because he is gracious. "God saved you by his grace when you believed. And you can't take credit for this; it is a gift from God. Salvation is not a reward for the good things we have done, so none of us can boast about it" (Ephesians 2:8–9).

Many people live a performance-based life. What they do determines the rewards or punishments they receive. Because of this perspective, they bring the scales of performance into their relationships. Are you living a performance-based life or is your life characterized by grace? How you honestly answer this question has a profound impact on your relationship with God and with others.

First, let's consider your relationship with God. Are you still trying to earn God's favor through your deeds? The Bible is clear that we will never be good enough to gain entrance into heaven apart from Jesus' saving grace. But even though believers rely on Christ's sacrifice for their salvation, later, like the Galatians, they often try to please God through their self-effort. In Galatians we read these words of challenge: "After starting your Christian lives in the Spirit, why are you now trying to become perfect by your own human effort?" (Galatians 3:3).

Certainly God wants us to live righteous lives and reflect Christ-like character qualities. We need to seek to live as Godly people. But the transformation of our character comes through our surrender to and dependence upon the Holy Spirit. Whatever blessings we receive are the result of God's loving-kindness.

So, what happens when you bring performance-oriented attitudes into human relationships? Acceptance is dependent upon behavior and rejection is the consequence of failing to satisfy the other person's expectations. As a result, there is insecurity and tension in these kinds of relationships.

> *"We must appropriate the tender mercy of God every day after conversion, or problems quickly develop. We need his daily grace in order to live a righteous life."*
>
> —David Jeremiah

God wants us to freely receive his grace and love. And he wants us to extend that same grace and love to others. In fact, with the help of the Holy Spirit, others may actually sense God's unconditional love and acceptance flowing through you.

With God as your Matchmaker, you need to remember that you do not have to be "good enough" to "earn" your soul mate. Instead, believe in God's goodness and expect him to give you far more than you deserve. I (Brad) can attest to this fact in my life. The many blessings I enjoy (including Nicole) are the result God's loving-kindness to me. Not because I have earned them.

Enjoy God's goodness and grace. It is really given freely.

QUESTIONS FROM THE MATCHMAKER

1. Honestly, in what ways are you deriving your value from a performance-based life? With me? With others?

2. What areas of your life are characterized by grace?

3. How can you appreciate more of my freely given grace?

AFFIRMATION

Heavenly Father, I want to embrace all of the good things in my life. I will focus on having them because you are good, not because I am worthy.

THE SECOND TIME AROUND

After you have worked through this devotional series the first time, go through the series again.

1. As you reflect on this devotion for a second time, do you have any new insights?

2. Since reading this devotion for the first time, have you identified any areas of your life where you are living in a performance-based way?

3. In what ways are you learning to live a more grace-filled life?

PART 3

YOUR DISCOVERY

OF YOUR

SOUL MATE

DAY 21
THE JOURNEY VS.
THE DESTINATION

"Go in peace. The LORD is watching over your journey."
Judges 18:6, BSB

When parents take their children on a trip, invariably they will hear the question, "Are we there yet?" In response, they encourage their kids to have patience and enjoy the ride. Yet often parents, during their own journey with God, ask a similar question, "What's taking so long?" Unfortunately, God never seems to be in a hurry.

So why are we in such a hurry? What's the rush in finding our soul mate and getting married sooner rather than later? Whether its marriage, a new job, or some other major goal, it's hard to wait for the rewards and benefits we are anticipating. We just know that we will be more happy, more secure, more valued, more loved, and more fulfilled once we "get there."

It's natural to want to get to our destination as soon as possible. But that is not God's priority. He is interested in the journey and what he will accomplish in us along the way. Even obstacles and delays serve in his ultimate purpose. Isaiah 55:8 tells us, "My thoughts are nothing like your thoughts," says the LORD. "And my ways are far beyond anything you could imagine."

Why is the journey so important to God?

Relationships take time and they deepen as we share experiences along the way. God uses our journey time with him to deepen his relationship with us individually. Things happen which cause us to share our thoughts, hopes, and feelings with him.

God also uses the journey time to develop our character. It's the potholes, detours, and difficulties along the way that provide opportunities to reshape and refine our attitudes and actions. When we finally arrive at our destination, God wants us to be thinking with his mindset. This takes time and it's his goal we not become derailed from his plan, but champions of endurance.

The apostle Paul reminds us, "We can rejoice, too, when we run into problems and trials, for we know that they help us develop endurance. And endurance develops strength of character, and character strengthens our confident hope of salvation" (Romans 5:3–4).

God is using the journey time to prepare the right setting and circumstances for our arrival at his destination. In his sovereignty, he is able to orchestrate events and arrange divine appointments. What seems like a delay or roadblock now may guarantee an exciting addition to our journey.

> *"Character can not be developed in ease and quiet. Only through experience of trial and suffering can the soul be strengthened, ambition inspired, and success achieved."*
>
> —Helen Keller

Don't be in a hurry. Trust God's pace for your journey. Along the way he is accomplishing much more than you could ever imagine. Remember these words from the Old Testament: "I will instruct you and teach you in the way you should go; I will counsel you with my loving eye on you" (Psalm 32:8, NIV).

QUESTIONS FROM THE MATCHMAKER

1. How can I help you focus on your journey toward finding a soul mate rather than just the destination?

2. What situation or circumstance in your life currently feels like a roadblock? Entrust it into my hands and trust my plan for you.

3. How has your character been developing recently? In what ways do you see me molding you?

AFFIRMATION

Heavenly Father, I will take time to enjoy my journey toward finding a soul mate rather than simply focusing on the final outcome.

THE SECOND TIME AROUND

After you have worked through this devotional series the first time, go through the series again.

1. As you reflect on this devotion for a second time, what new insights do you have?

2. Which one of the Matchmaker's questions (preceding page) is most relevant to you at this point in your life?

3. In what ways are you appreciating the journey toward finding a soulmate?

DAY 22
THE GOAL OF ONENESS

Do not be yoked together with unbelievers.
For what do righteousness and wickedness have in common?
Or what fellowship can light have with darkness?
2 Corinthians 6:14, NIV

Let's go back in time. In fact, let's go all the way back to before the beginning of creation when there was only a triune God. There was only one will—God's will.

Then God created angels. Eventually, the supreme angel Lucifer chose to step outside of God's will. He decided to exert his own distorted will in opposition to God's will. Now there were two wills at war in the universe.

Later God created Adam and Eve as perfect humans. But through the deception of Satan, Adam and Eve disobeyed God and exerted their self-will—now there were multiple conflicting wills in the universe.

Today the world is filled with self-willed people. The result is self-centeredness, hostility, and conflict.

And yet, all of creation and history exist for the glory of God. In Revelation 4:11 we read these words: "You are worthy, our Lord and God, to receive glory and honor and power, for you created all things, and by your will they were created and have their being" (NIV).

Through Jesus Christ, God has made it possible for us to once again experience oneness and peace with him.

How's your relationship with God? Are you experiencing oneness with him? Or is there disagreement and conflict resulting from differences in what you want versus what God wants? Your ultimate happiness and fulfillment are only possible as you get into alignment with your creator God.

As you seek a soul mate, don't settle for just peace or harmony in your relationship. Set your sights on unity and oneness with your mate. Peace is the absence of conflict, which usually comes about through tolerance or avoidance. Harmony becomes possible through cooperation and respect for each other's roles and differences. It involves respect, trust, and support. However, it still falls short of the ideal of unity and oneness.

> *"Unity does not mean sameness. It means oneness of purpose."*
>
> —Priscilla Shirer

So how can that be achieved? As believers, our common ground becomes the oneness we share with God. Through that oneness, we can share unity with other believers, but more importantly, oneness with our soul mate.

Oneness is only possible through the working of the Holy Spirit in our lives. He is the one who helps transform our attitude and will so we learn to think as God does. Ephesians 4:2–3 tells us, "Be completely humble and gentle; be patient, bearing with one another in love. Make every effort to keep the unity of the Spirit through the bond of peace" (NIV).

Oneness requires genuine love, like-mindedness, and singularity of purpose. Paul encourages us to be, "of one mind, having the same love, being united in spirit and purpose" (Philippians 2:2, BSB).

God desires oneness for you and your soul mate. Obviously, this is only possible if both of you have received Jesus into your lives as your Lord and Savior and are pursuing an ever-closer relationship with God. In reality, the closer both of you are to God, the closer you will be able to be with each other. As your wills are yielded to God's desires, your self-centeredness will be replaced with humility, love, and unity.

Wait for God's best. Wait for a soul mate with whom you can enjoy God's unity and oneness.

QUESTIONS FROM THE MATCHMAKER

1. In what ways are you experiencing oneness with me?

2. What characteristics are important to you as you consider experiencing oneness with a soul mate?

3. What are you currently struggling with yielding to me? Trust me to know what is best for you.

AFFIRMATION

Sovereign God, I commit myself to experiencing oneness with my soul mate and not settling for anything less.

THE SECOND TIME AROUND

After you have worked through this devotional series the first time, go through the series again.

1. As you reflect on this devotion for a second time, in what new ways are you experiencing oneness with God?

2. What are you learning about what it means to have oneness in a relationship?

3. What is changing in you or your circumstances?

DAY 23
CHARACTER MATTERS

You can identify them by their fruit, that is, by the way they act.
Can you pick grapes from thorn bushes, or figs from thistles?
Matthew 7:16

Character is the essence of who we are. Our character is comprised of the values and convictions that have been shaped by our relationships and life experiences. Character is developed over time.

All too often, when someone is seeking their soul mate, they focus on external qualities and do not pay enough attention to character. What does this person look like? What kind of job/car/house does this person have? They assume that character issues can be adjusted later. The flaw with this approach however, is character changes usually require a great deal of time. Which means that the character qualities you see while dating are typically what you will be living with after marriage.

Every person has external and internal qualities. The external are easily perceived, but the inner qualities require careful observation. When the prophet Samuel was sent by God to anoint a new king of Israel to replace Saul, God cautioned him, "Don't judge by his appearance or height, for I have rejected him. The LORD doesn't see things the way you see them.

> *"There is no way to grow a saint overnight. Character, like the oak tree, does not spring up like a mushroom."*
> —Vance Havner

People judge by outward appearance, but the LORD looks at the heart" (1 Samuel 16:7).

God is not only concerned about the character of your future soul mate—he is also concerned about your character development. He wants to deal with whatever critical changes are necessary in both of you before bringing the two of you together. Here are some guidelines you can use to review yourself and to help you discern the character in others.

Words reflect inner self.

It's not what goes into your mouth that defiles you; you are defiled by the words that come out of your mouth.
> —Matthew 15:11

Actions speak louder than words.

A good tree can't produce bad fruit, and a bad tree can't produce good fruit.
> —Luke 6:43

Friendships indicate standards.

Do not be misled: "Bad company corrupts good character."
> —Corinthians 15:33, NIV

Expenditures demonstrate values.

Wherever your treasure is, there the desires of your heart will also be.
> —Matthew 6:21

Difficulties reveal strength (and weakness) of character.

We can rejoice, too, when we run into problems and trials, for we know that they help us develop endurance. And endurance develops strength of character.

— Romans 5:3–4

Character is who you really are. Whenever God reveals something in your character that he wants to change, stop and ask the Holy Spirit to help bring about the necessary transformation.

QUESTIONS FROM THE MATCHMAKER

1. Think for a moment about your past attitudes and behaviors and the impact they have had on your character. What past situations do you need me to free you from?

2. Honestly, in what ways do you tend to focus on external qualities rather than internal character? How can I help you?

3. What character qualities do you think exhibit spiritual maturity?

AFFIRMATION

Father God, I will seek a soul mate of integrity and good character.

THE SECOND TIME AROUND

After you have worked through this devotional series the first time, go through the series again.

1. As you reflect on this devotion for a second time, do you have any new insights?

2. Would you answer any of the Questions from the Match-maker (preceding page) differently now than when you first read this devotion?

3. In what ways is your character deepening?

DAY 24
DON'T MAKE ASSUMPTIONS

Can two people walk together without agreeing on the direction?
Amos 3:3

Assumptions. We all make them. Some of our assumptions are right and some are wrong. But we usually don't realize an assumption is wrong until it is too late and we've stepped into the future with faulty information.

We often assume facts about our circumstances, other people, and God. And those assumptions move us forward with a belief for an accepted outcome. When what we believed turns out to be inaccurate, we are typically filled with disappointment.

No doubt there have been times when you were sure you knew what God was going to do. But then things turned out differently than you expected. Maybe you were left confused and wondering why God would allow something seemingly bad to happen. Other times you may have been surprised because God did what you anticipated, but in a way that was completely unexpected.

God told the prophet Isaiah, "For my thoughts are not your thoughts, neither are your ways my ways" (Isaiah 55:8, NIV). When you think about that verse, it makes sense. God has abilities far beyond ours and sees things from a very different perspective than ours.

Nonetheless, we still fall into the trap of expecting God to do things in a way that makes sense to us. We also expect others to share our assumptions and expectations.

We seldom remember that our personal thought patterns and habits are unique. Our individual life experiences, relationships and education have helped to make us the distinct people that we are. And yet, we still assume that other individuals will share our personal viewpoints and handle situations the way we would.

In the excitement of a new relationship, individuals often fail to discuss life expectations. It's just fun to be together.

> *"Assumption: A fact or statement taken for granted."*
>
> —Miriam-Webster

However, at some point, it's important to have a discussion about personal expectations. If this relationship leads to marriage, what are your expectations within the relationship? Are you both going to work? What about children? How about finances? Are you willing to make a career change or geographical move? What about your spiritual life? Is church attendance important? What church will you attend? Will you pray together? How do your faith journeys intersect?

Many people make assumptions about the answers to these questions based on how they grew up and what their parents modeled. Because the answers seem obvious or "normal" to them, they may not even think to talk about these issues. But all of these issues are critical to a compatible relationship down the road.

Take time to talk about the goals of your life … and listen carefully to the person you are dating as they talk about their goals and expectations. Nothing is too small that it shouldn't be shared and discussed.

QUESTIONS FROM THE MATCHMAKER

1. What are some of the expectations you are bringing to a relationship with your soul mate?

2. How can I help you to clarify your goals for a lifelong relationship?

3. What assumptions about me do you need to have clarified?

AFFIRMATION

Heavenly Father, I will accept that everyone does not see life the way I do.

THE SECOND TIME AROUND

After you have worked through this devotional series the first time, go through the series again.

1. Since reading this devotion for the first time, in what ways are you identifying areas of your life that have incorrect assumptions?

2. What is God teaching you about assumptions?

3. What is changing in your relationships as you remember to not make assumptions?

DAY 25
A Thankful Heart

Be thankful in all circumstances,
for this is God's will for you who belong to Christ Jesus.
1 Thessalonians 5:18

Are you a glass half-full or a glass half-empty type person? We all have different personalities. Some of us have a naturally more positive outlook on life, while others quickly see the downside of any given situation. But regardless of how we were designed, God wants to cultivate a gratitude-filled heart within each of us. Thankfulness is mentioned in many New Testament passages that focus on the Holy Spirit's role in our lives.

So how can we cooperate with the Holy Spirit to develop a consistent attitude of gratitude?

1. Choose to look at life with a gratitude perspective.

Thankfulness is a choice. It is intentional. You can't experience gratitude if you are focusing on negative circumstances. Regardless of your difficulties, God is still a loving, good God.

> Give thanks for everything to God the Father in the name of our Lord Jesus Christ.
>
> —Ephesians 5:20

> *"The joy of the Holy Spirit is experienced by giving thanks in all situations."*
>
> —Bill Bright

There is always someone who you believe is better off than you. And there is always someone you know who has it worse. The joy of the Holy Spirit is experienced by giving thanks in all situations. The secret to living a life of gratitude is not to covet someone who has more but to be content with what God has chosen to give you.

2. Look for signs of God's love and goodness to you.

Ask the Holy Spirit to open your spiritual eyes so you can see what God is doing in your life right now. Watch for his fingerprints on your daily activities as he orchestrates events and guides your footsteps.

> May you be filled with joy, always thanking the Father.
> —Colossians 1:12

Make it a habit to thank God for all that you notice as being unique in your day. Be alert and anticipate God's involvement in your daily life. As you focus on his presence, the Holy Spirit will open your eyes to show you what God is doing in your life.

3. Meditate on God's mercy, loving-kindness, and goodness.

There are times when we feel we deserve better. In reality, looking through God's divine standards of holiness and right-eousness, we deserve far less. It is only because of God's grace and Christ's sacrifice for us that we can enjoy blessings that will last for eternity.

> Give thanks to the LORD, for he is good! His faithful love endures forever.
> —Psalm 107:1

Be content with where you are and with what you have. When your life is characterized by a heart that overflows with gratitude to God for his goodness, you are the kind of person other people enjoy. Ask God to give you a heart of gratitude so others (and your soul mate) will enjoy being in your presence. Develop a habit of thankfulness and contentment.

QUESTIONS FROM THE MATCHMAKER

1. In what area of your life would you like to see your attitude change from anxiousness to expectancy? Do this by watching for me throughout your day.

2. If you don't see your life as good, maybe your definition of goodness, is not mine. As you consider your life from my perspective, what is currently good?

3. How can I help you develop a heart of contentment?

AFFIRMATION

All-loving God, I will think daily about your mercy, goodness, and loving-kindness.

THE SECOND TIME AROUND

After you have worked through this devotional series the first time, go through the series again.

1. As you reflect on this devotion for a second time, do you have any new insights?

2. In what ways does your attitude currently reveal content-ment?

3. As an exercise in thankfulness, take time each day for the next week to write down 10 things for which you are thankful.

DAY 26
UNCONDITIONAL LOVE

Above all, love each other deeply,
because love covers over a multitude of sins.
1 Peter 4:8, NIV

Have you ever heard, "I will love you if …" expressed either in words or by someone's actions? In either case, you got the message. Love for you was based on conditions. If you met the conditions, you would receive love. If you failed, you weren't worthy of love.

The world operates on performance-based love. And unfortunately, that is how most of us unwittingly live. But God offers us a different way to experience love and to share love.

"God loves me if …"

What do you believe about God's love for you? Do you feel like God loves you more when you are good and less when you are disobedient? The truth is, we do not deserve God's love. There is nothing we can do to earn it. It is freely given to us because that is God's very nature. We are beneficiaries of God's love because of Christ's death for us on the cross.

The apostle Paul explains, "Nothing can ever separate us from God's love" (Romans 8:38). Is there anything that "nothing" does not encompass? Consider Jesus' parable of the Lost Son (see Luke 15:11-32). This boy squandered his inherit-ance in reckless living. Yes, his father was disappointed and heartbroken by his son's choices, but he never stopped loving his son and he welcomed him home with open arms.

> *"You can always give without loving, but you can never love without giving."*
> —Amy Carmichael

God loves you unconditionally and will do so forever. However, uncondi-tional love should not be equated with unconditional acceptance of behavior. God loves each and every sinner but hates our sin. Hebrews 12 tells us that God will discipline us in love as a Father disciplines his child.

"I love me if ..."

How do you feel about yourself? Do you struggle with self-condemnation when you do not live up to your own expecta-tions and standards? If you have accepted the pardon for your sins that Jesus purchased for you on the cross, "there is now no condemnation for (you) those who are in Christ Jesus" (Romans 8:1, NIV). God wants you to hate your sin—not condone it. But he does not want you to live a life of self-condemnation. Confess your sin to God, repent of it, and then ask the Holy Spirit to help you see yourself as the forgiven, loved child you now are in Christ.

"I love you if ..."

Do you make others feel like they need to perform in order to receive your love? You were created in the image of God and God is love (1 John 4:16). He wants you to be a vessel through whom he can love others around you. That is only possible to the degree that the Holy Spirit radiates the love of Jesus through you.

Ephesians 5:1–2 tells us, "Therefore be imitators of God as dear children. And walk in love, as Christ also has loved us and given Himself for us" (NKJV).

You are to be Christ's mouth, hands, and feet so others can see Jesus in you and feel his love through you. That is God's desire for you. "May the Lord make your love increase and overflow for each other and for everyone else, just as ours does for you" (1 Thessalonians 3:12, NIV).

QUESTIONS FROM THE MATCHMAKER

1. What is standing in the way of you accepting my love for you?

2. My love is meant to transform your thinking and then your way of life. In what ways will allowing my love to change your thinking cause you to think differently about yourself?

3. How will my love enable you to think differently about the people around you?

AFFIRMATION

Loving God, I accept the full power of your transforming love.

THE SECOND TIME AROUND

After you have worked through this devotional series the first time, go through the series again.

1. As you reflect on this devotion for a second time, in what new ways are you experiencing God's unconditional love?

2. Would you answer any of the Matchmaker's questions differently now?

3. In what ways is God's love flowing through you to those around you?

DAY 27
FEAR NOT

Be strong and courageous. Do not be afraid or terrified because of them, for the LORD your God goes with you; he will never leave you nor forsake you.

Deuteronomy 31:6, NIV

What is it you fear? Is it rejection? Failure to find someone? A marriage that will not last?

I (Brad) was divorced after many years of marriage. When I got married the first time, I believed it would last forever. But things happen, people change and commitments are broken. My greatest fear when considering the possibility of remarriage was that my marriage could fail again. I wanted a guarantee that I would not experience another broken marriage relationship. But there are no guarantees. In any marriage, when people drift away from God, they enter a place where they are just one bad decision away from disaster.

> *"Our future may look fearfully intimidating, yet we can look up to the engineer of the universe confident nothing escapes his attention or slips out of the control of those strong hands."*
>
> —Elizabeth Elliot

Is fear holding you back in pursuing a significant relationship? The Bible tells us, "God has not given us a spirit of fear and timidity, but of power, love, and self-discipline" (2 Timothy 1:7).

When we live with a spirit of fear, our minds are filled with every imaginable bad thing that could happen. We don't want to move forward until we have assurance everything is safe. Only God can take away fear, he is the answer!

Fear of Being Hurt

No one wants to experience pain, whether physically or emotionally. But we can all become more courageous as we shift our gaze to our loving, powerful heavenly Father.

> The LORD is my light and my salvation—so why should I be afraid? The LORD is my fortress, protecting me from danger, so why should I tremble?
> —Psalm 27:1

God provides us with his light so we can become aware of real danger, instead of imagined danger, as we move forward.

Fear of Rejection

Venturing into new relationships can be unnerving because we cannot be sure of how we will be received by others. Rejection is painful. But when we keep our focus on God and his unconditional love for us, what others think becomes less important.

> We can say with confidence, 'The LORD is my helper, so I will have no fear. What can mere people do to me?'
> —Hebrews 13:6

When you experience "rejection," remember that that person is not God's match for you. Be thankful that it was made clear so you can go forward on your journey to his best.

Fear of Abandonment

We desire faithfulness and security in relationships. But, sometimes people disappoint us with their lack of commitment. However, God is still with us.

> "For I hold you by your right hand—I, the LORD your God. And I say to you, 'Don't be afraid. I am here to help you.'"
>
> —Isaiah 41:13

God's commitment to you will never falter.

Don't let your fear prevent you from moving forward. Share your fears with God and ask him to replace them with confidence in his loving care for you. Psalm 34:4 assures us, "I prayed to the LORD, and he answered me. He freed me from all my fears."

QUESTIONS FROM THE MATCHMAKER

1. What fears do you have concerning your soul mate that you need to give to me?

2. How can my attributes of love and faithfulness change how your see your present situation in life?

3. What are you seeking to control in your life right now that you need to turn over to me?

AFFIRMATION

All-powerful God, I will trust you in all things.

THE SECOND TIME AROUND

After you have worked through this devotional series the first time, go through the series again.

1. As you reflect on this devotion for a second time, do you have any new insights about what you fear and how you can handle that fear?

2. In what ways are you handling your fears differently than you have in the past?

3. What is changing in you and your circumstances?

DAY 28
A Perseverance Mindset

Let's not get tired of doing what is good. At just the right time
we will reap a harvest of blessing if we don't give up.
Galatians 6:9

D o you ever feel like just giving up? I (Brad) sure had those feelings many times when I re-entered the dating scene after being divorced. Sometimes other well-meaning people said things to me that were actually quite discouraging. Those were times when I wanted to give up because I could not see any way my desire for marriage could become a reality. I felt like it was hopeless. But God knew Nicole was waiting for me.

Why does this journey have to be so difficult?
God permits trials for our development.

> Dear brothers and sisters, when troubles of any kind come your way, consider it an opportunity for great joy. For you know that when your faith is tested, your endurance has a chance to grow. So let it grow, for when your endurance is fully developed, you will be perfect and complete, needing nothing.
>
> —James 1:2–4

Difficulties are an opportunity for us to lean into God's care

> *"Never be afraid to hope—or ask for a miracle."*
>
> —Criswell Freeman

and strength. The more we focus on God's abilities and commitment to us, the more our faith in him increases. And we keep moving forward. Trials are intended to strengthen our faith and increase our perseverance. With fully developed perseverance, we become all God planned for us to be in Christ.

Why is perseverance so important?
Perseverance builds character and strong character produces confident hope.

> We can rejoice, too, when we run into problems and trials, for we know that they help us develop endurance. And endurance develops strength of character, and character strengthens our confident hope of salvation.
> —Romans 5:3–4

With hope, we can envision the fulfillment of God's promises as we focus on what he has said and his trustworthy character. And the result is joy and peace.

Hope overcomes discouragement and enables us to persevere.
Sometimes our situation can seem overwhelming. We may even think it is pointless to go on. But the real problem is that we are focused on our circumstances instead of God.

> Why am I discouraged? Why is my heart so sad? I will put my hope in God! I will praise him again—my Savior and my God!
> —Psalm 43:5

Every person on this earth will encounter times of discouragement. The only way to get out of a dark pit is to look up to God.

No one who trusts in you will ever be disgraced … Lead me by your truth and teach me, for you are the God who saves me. All day long I put my hope in you.

—Psalm 25:3,5

"But those who trust in the LORD will find new strength. They will soar high on wings like eagles. They will run and not grow weary. They will walk and not faint."

—Isaiah 40:31

God is working in you. Hold on to him as you continue your journey to find a soul mate. He is developing your character and preparing you to be the right soul mate for someone.

QUESTIONS FROM THE MATCHMAKER

1. I have not called you to a life of being overwhelmed. Give me your weariness and I, in turn, will give you strength. Where in your life would you like to be filled with my strength?

2. How can I help you experience joy in your perseverance?

3. What situation in your life do you need to turn over to me?

AFFIRMATION

Lord, I will lean into your strength at all times.

The Second Time Around

After you have worked through this devotional series the first time, go through the series again.

1. Since reading this devotion for the first time, how have you grown in perseverance?

2. In what ways is God molding your character through the difficulties in your life? What are you learning about him?

3. How do you see God preparing you to be the right soul mate for someone?

DAY 29
SEEK DIVINE GUIDANCE

Since we are living by the Spirit,
let us follow the Spirit's leading in every part of our lives.
Galatians 5:25

The Matchmaker wants to guide you on your journey, but do you know how to discern his direction? How do you separate what God is saying to you from all the other distracting messages around you?

First, prepare your heart to hear God.

✦ By getting right with God.

> If we confess our sins, he is faithful and just and will forgive us our sins and purify us from all unrighteousness.
>
> —1 John 1:9, NIV

✦ By surrendering your will to God.

> We know that God does not listen to sinners. He listens to the godly man who does his will.
>
> —John 9:31, NIV

✦ By humbling yourself before God.

> And what does the LORD require of you? To act justly and to love mercy and to walk humbly with your God.
> —Micah 6:8, NIV

✦ By renewing your mind with biblical truth.

> Be transformed by the renewing of your mind. Then you will be able to test and approve what God's will is—his good, pleasing and perfect will.
> —Romans 12:2, NIV

✦ By having a mindset of faith, trust, and expectancy toward God.

> We live by faith, not by sight.
> —2 Corinthians 5:7, NIV

✦ By being patient and willing to wait on God.

> Wait for the LORD; be strong and take heart and wait for the LORD.
> —Psalm 27:14

Second, monitor God's channels of communication.

✦ God directs our steps through his Word, the Bible.

> Your word is a lamp to my feet and a light for my path.
> —Psalm 119:105, NIV

✦ God directs our steps through the prompting of the Holy Spirit.

> But when he, the Spirit of truth, comes, he will guide you into all truth.
> —John 16:13, NIV

✦ God directs our steps through other people.

> Make plans by seeking advice.
> —Proverbs 20:18, NIV

✦ God directs our steps through providential circumstances.

> But Joseph said ... "You intended to harm me, but God intended it for good to accomplish what is now being done, the saving of many lives."
> —Genesis 50:19–20, NIV

Third, make sure the direction is from God.

✦ Does it comply with the directions given in God's written Word?

> Direct my footsteps according to your word; let no sin rule over me.
> —Psalm 119:133

✦ Does it make sense when you use sanctified reasoning that is based on God's truth?

> Do not conform any longer to the pattern of this world, but be transformed by the renewing of your mind. Then you will be able to test and approve what God's will is—his good, pleasing and perfect will.
> —Romans 12:2, NIV

✦ Does it seem to fit with the surrounding circumstances?

> In him we were also chosen, having been predestined according to the plan of him who works out everything in conformity with the purpose of his will.
> —Ephesians 1:11, NIV

✦ Does it concur with the advice you have received from wise godly counselors?

> Plans fail for lack of counsel, but with many advisers they succeed.
> —Proverbs 15:22, NIV

✦ Does it generate a supernatural inner peace and calmness that cannot be attributed to your circumstances?

> Do not be anxious about anything, but in everything, by prayer and petition, with thanksgiving, present your requests to God. And the peace of God, which transcends all understanding, will guard your hearts and your minds in Christ Jesus.
> —Philippians 4:6–7, NIV

You do not have to be able to answer "yes" to all of the preceding questions to confirm the direction as being from God. However, if you answer "no" to any of these questions, wait on God to give you more confirmation before taking action.

Fourth, trust God to guide you.

✦ Believe God will give you the wisdom you need.

> If any of you lacks wisdom, he should ask God, who gives generously to all without finding fault, and it will be given to him.
> —James 1:5, NIV

✦ Rely on God to show you the right way.

> I will instruct you and teach you in the way you should go; I will counsel you and watch over you.
> —Psalm 32:8, NIV

✦ Expect God to confirm or redirect your steps.

> In his heart a man plans his course, but the LORD determines his steps.
> —Proverbs 16:9, NIV

Discovering God's will and discerning his direction is more dependent on your relationship with him than a process of steps. He wants to guide you. Stay close to him. Hear his words. Notice his signs. He will reveal his plan to you at the right time.

QUESTIONS FROM THE MATCHMAKER

1. When have you approached my Word with a specific need and almost had a passage jump off the page at you in response to that need? If not, ask me to do that for you now.

2. When did you have an inner impression or feeling that you sensed may have been me trying to direct your steps? Did you follow the urgings? Prepare your heart to follow the next promptings.

3. When have you listened to someone and suddenly it was as if I were speaking through them to you about your situation?

AFFIRMATION

Heavenly Father, I will daily watch for and then follow the Holy Spirit's direction.

THE SECOND TIME AROUND

After you have worked through this devotional series the first time, go through the series again.

1. Since reading this devotion for the first time, when have you noticed events or circumstances that seemed to be orchestrated by God trying to direct your steps?

2. Through which channels of communication have you noticed God giving you guidance?

3. In what areas of your life do you see God giving you guidance right now? Are you following his direction?

DAY 30
ASK, SEEK, KNOCK

Ask and it will be given to you; seek and you will find;
knock and the door will be opened to you.
Matthew 7:7, NIV

God wants us to involve him in the pursuit of our desires. In the Sermon on the Mount, Jesus reveals a simple but profound three-step process to help us: ask, seek, and knock.

When we are looking for our soul mate, we usually change this sequence. First we begin by seeking. Then we knock on various doors to see if any will open. And then finally, we ask a person hoping to get the answer we desire.

I (Brad) remember thinking that Jesus made a mistake with this sequence. Why did he begin with "ask"? The answer is actually quite obvious. Jesus is not talking about asking a person. He is telling us to ask God before we even begin seeking and knocking.

1. Ask

Have you ever asked someone you didn't know for something significant? If so, deep down you probably doubted you would get what you wanted. That's because usually the depth of relationship needs to be in proportion to the size of the request.

125

Jesus tells us to ask our heavenly Father (see Matthew 7:9–11). We begin by asking him for the things we desire. We go to him because we know he cares. We go to him because he wants to be involved in our lives.

Prayer changes things in the spiritual realm when we ask according to God's guidelines (see 1 John 5:14–15; Matthew 21:22; James 4:3; 1 John 3:21–22; John 15:7; John 15:16; Luke 18:1,6–8). However, it may take time before that change becomes noticeable in the physical realm. By faith, make it a habit to thank God for his answer while you wait for its manifestation.

> *"We cannot rely on God's promises without obeying his commandments."*
>
> —John Calvin

Demonstrate your faith and anticipation by "seeking" and "knocking."

2. Seek

Why does God want us to seek after asking him for what we desire? Seeking implies faith and expectation. Do you believe in God's ability to fulfill your desire? Are you trusting that he cares enough about you to follow through? Are your motives for the request according to God standards?

Work through whatever issues you may have so that you can actively watch and expect God to act on your behalf. The apostle Paul tells us, "Devote yourselves to prayer, being watchful and thankful" (Colossians 4:2, NIV).

Look for possible ways through which God may answer your prayer. With an attitude of expectation and anticipation, be sensitive to the Holy Spirit. Stay alert; if you believe God has answered your prayer, you will be looking for its manifestation.

3. Knock

God doesn't just want you to watch for opportunities expectantly, he also wants you to put feet to your faith. As the Holy

Spirit makes you aware of possibilities, be faithful to pursue them. Knock on the door of a possibility to see if it will open wide or slam shut.

What God doesn't answer immediately he will answer eventually. As you walk by faith, continue to thank God for his answer. Although you do not know when it will arrive, it will be on schedule according to his timetable. Keep on thanking him for his promise: "For everyone who asks receives, he who seeks finds; and to him who knocks, the door will be opened" (Matthew 7:8, NIV).

QUESTIONS FROM THE MATCHMAKER

1. What are you presently asking me for?

2. In what ways are you seeking?

3. In what ways are you knocking?

AFFIRMATION

Gracious God, with anticipation and thanksgiving I will ask you to open the right doors for me.

THE SECOND TIME AROUND

After you have worked through this devotional series the first time, go through the series again.

1. As you reflect on this devotion for a second time, do you have any new insights?

2. What are you learning about how to "ask, seek, and knock"?

3. In what ways is the "ask, seek, and knock" approach to life changing you? Changing your circumstances?

DAY 31
THE NEXT FAITH STEP

We can make our plans, but the LORD determines our steps.
Proverbs 16:9

Where do you go from here? Perhaps you are the kind of person who likes to plan everything out. You want to know the exact route to your destination and make sure you have everything you need before you embark on your way. Or maybe you are a free spirit who feels comfortable letting life happen without much forethought.

God wants you to walk into your future by faith with him. What does that mean? You will not know exactly where the road will take you. And you will not be able to count on your resources or abilities to get you to your destination. And the destination that you have chosen may even be changed!

Two Corinthians 5:7 tells us, "For we walk by faith, not by sight" (BSB). God wants you to walk into the future knowing that he is by your side and trusting in his goodness. He is your guide, companion, provider, and protector. He wants you to trust him because you know him and have a history of adventures with him. You don't know what the future holds. You don't know what lies around the next bend of life. But he does. And he is committed to caring for you as you walk the road together.

We don't know what the next step for you might be. I (Brad) met several wonderful Christian women during the years I was seeking my soul mate. And many times I felt sure where the path would lead only to be surprised and disappointed. But the Matchmaker was guiding. He was preparing me to be the person I needed to be before I met Nicole. He was refining and fashioning each of us for each other so the fit would be ideal. And that is what we have discovered. We are so grateful for the Matchmaker's commitment to our ultimate best, even though that meant difficult and disappointing times along the way.

> "God uses our most stumbling, faltering faith-steps as the open door to His doing for us 'more than we ask or think."
> —Catherine Marshall

It's true that the journey ahead of you might be longer than you wish. You may go through dark valleys. There might be detours and cliffs on either side of the road. Whatever the case may be, it's okay. If you just do the next step, you will get there. Are you feeling nervous right now? Discouraged even? Trust that God hasn't forgotten you. He's right here with you—listening to you, loving you, desiring a closer relationship with you. Lean on his Word and his understanding in times of seeming hopelessness, and he will provide you with the love, strength, and encouragement you need to take the next step.

God is more capable and involved in guiding your steps and orchestrating your circumstances than you can imagine. King Solomon wrote, "A person's steps are directed by the LORD. How then can anyone understand their own way?" (Proverbs 20:24). Take your next step by faith, knowing that God will redirect you if necessary. You can go forward with this assurance: "The Lord himself goes before you and will be with you; he will never leave you nor forsake you. Do not be afraid; do not be discouraged" (Deuteronomy 31:8)

So, what is your next decision to make? What is the next step to take? Whatever it is, do it. God will be there with you. He is your partner on this journey.

QUESTIONS FROM THE MATCHMAKER

1. Today, what do you need to entrust into my hands?

2. Remember, I am with you—listening to you, loving you, desiring a closer relationship with you. What is it that you most need from me?

3. What times in the past have I shown you clearly which way to go?

AFFIRMATION

Heavenly Father, I will embrace where you are leading, even though it may not be in the direction I have in mind.

THE SECOND TIME AROUND

After you have worked through this devotional series the first time, go through the series again.

1. As you have read through this devotion a second time, what stands out most to you today?

2. In what ways are you currently experiencing the Matchmaker's presence and guidance in your life?

3. In what ways are you becoming more of who you believe God wants you to be in order to be a perfect soul mate?

Conclusion
The Journey continues

You have come to the end of this devotional series, but do not let this be the end of your journey with the Matchmaker. In fact, it would be beneficial to go through these devotions a second time. See what has changed in your life and in your relationship with God. See what still needs reinforcement.

Remember that each relationship God allows into your life is his personal gift to you. He is bringing people into your life for your further development as well as theirs.

My last relationship before I met Brad had become quite serious. I was in an emotionally needy place and guess who I attracted? Someone else who was emotional needy! My boyfriend and I went to church and bible study together and enjoyed the process of getting to know God better. There was such good spiritual compatibility, and based on that, he started pushing for marriage.

The eagerness to marry became understandable when I stumbled upon the fact he was carrying emotional baggage that affected how he interacted with the people closest to him as well as how he managed money.

Even though I had strong ties spiritually with him, these issues became a deal breaker for me. I felt God release me from going further. It had been a whirlwind relationship, one that I acknowledged God wanted me to pursue, but it wasn't for the sake of marriage. It was because my boyfriend needed someone to care for him while the truth was exposed.

That experience embarrassed him, but because he was committed to God's revelation in his life, this situation also freed him from the fear of exposure. He was able to release the emotions that were holding him in bondage. As a result, he began the process of learning how to replace his emotional baggage with the peace of God.

I was relieved to be out of what had become a pressure situation. But I have no doubt that it was God who brought us together for a season so that his work in my life, as well as my boyfriend's life, could be accomplished.

We have learned to believe that God is working through current situations to bring you to your soul mate, one relationship at a time.

> Now to Him who is able to do exceedingly abundantly above all that we ask or think, according to the power that works in us.
> —Ephesians 3:20, NKJV

Trust God more and rely on yourself less. He is able. He is willing. He is trustworthy. Spend time with him every day so your trust in him will grow.

Enjoy your adventure with the ultimate Matchmaker.

Brad and Nicole

APPENDIX

Affirmations

1. Almighty God, I choose to walk with you by faith on this supernatural journey so you can unveil your ideal plan for me.

2. Heavenly Father, I embrace your unconditional, unstoppable, unfathomable love for me as I am blessed by your goodness towards me everyday.

3. Father, help me to learn to hear your voice, and help me to feel the peace and power that comes from trusting your plans for me.

4. Almighty God, I trust you to do the impossible regardless of my limited understanding, ability, and resources.

5. Faithful Father, I choose to trust you for what seems impossible, even though I can't see how it will be accomplished.

6. Loving Father, I will pursue a deeper relationship with you by reading your words in the Bible, watching for signs of your goodness, and living with a more conscious awareness of your loving presence.

7. Father God, I know that you are at work to create the ultimate best for me.

8. Sovereign God, I trust in the perfectness of your timing even though it is hard for me to wait.

9. Heavenly Father, I will talk with you about everything because I know you hear me.

10. Sovereign Lord, I am excited to see the new things you are doing and will bring about in my life.

11. Father God, I embrace the fact that my past doesn't have to dictate my future because I am a new person in Jesus Christ.

12. Heavenly Father, I choose your perspective even when it might be difficult to embrace. I know that you see and know all things and you have my very best interests in mind.

13. Father God, you have given me your Word and your Spirit to help me know your will for my life. I want to be transformed by your power working in me.

14. Heavenly Father, because you have placed such a high priority on developing a relationship with me, I will honor you by placing a high priority on our relationship as well. I want to keep you as first place in my life always.

15. All knowing God, I choose to embrace thoughts that are from you and reject those that are in opposition to your values, ways, and purposes.

16. Gracious heavenly Father, I choose to rely on you when the adversities of life press in on me.

17. Gracious God, I will focus on the possibilities of the present and not be guilt-ridden by habits or mistakes I have made in the past. I entrust my future into your hands.

18. Faithful God, with your help, I will honor the commitments I have, even when they are not convenient or require sacrifice.

19. Creator God, I am a beautiful person because you made me!

20. Heavenly Father, I want to embrace all of the good things in my life. I will focus on having them because you are good, not because I am worthy.

21. Heavenly Father, I will take time to enjoy my journey toward finding a soul mate rather than simply focusing on the final outcome.

22. Sovereign God, I commit myself to experiencing oneness with my soul mate and not settling for anything less.

23. Father God, I will seek a soul mate of integrity and good character.

24. Heavenly Father, I will accept that everyone does not see life the way I do.

25. All-loving God, I will think daily about your mercy, goodness, and loving-kindness.

26. God, I accept the full power of your transforming love.

27. All-powerful God, I will trust you in all things.

28. Lord, I will lean into your strength at all times.

29. Heavenly Father, I will daily watch for and then follow the Holy Spirit's direction.

30. Gracious God, with anticipation and thanksgiving I will ask you to open the right doors for me.

31. Heavenly Father, I will embrace where you are leading, even though it may not be in the direction I have in mind.

Related Book

Soul Mates by God:
Let God be Your Matchmaker

Many single people are deep in doubt that they'll ever find the right person. Does that include you? Are you looking for that special someone? Maybe you've never been married. Perhaps your marriage ended in death or divorce. And yet, you still long to share your life with that special soul mate.

If you desire to find that unique person with whom you can spend the rest of your life, then *Soul Mates by God* can help.

Begin Your Adventure with God
- Take three tests to gain clarity about God's plan for you.
- Make sure you're on the right path to receive God's best.
- Become the right person so you can meet the right person.

Unload Your Baggage
- Don't let your past jeopardize your future.
- Develop the right reasons for wanting to marry.
- Learn from the past to prepare for the future.

Focus Your Dating Strategy
- Avoid the "type" trap.
- Think about "compatibility."
- Know where to "circulate."

Soul Mates by God is a life transforming dating guide for Christians. Discover principles and insights in how to cooperate with the greatest Matchmaker of all time.

SoulMatesByGod.com
ISBN: 978-1541343634
$19.99 US